# RELIGIOUS WOMEN
# IN THE MODERN WORLD

# Religious Women
# in the Modern World

*Judith Tate*

HERDER AND HERDER

1970
HERDER AND HERDER NEW YORK
232 Madison Avenue, New York, N.Y. 10016

*Nihil obstat:* Brendan W. Lawlor, Censor Librorum
*Imprimatur:* ✝Robert F. Joyce, Bishop of Burlington
April 3, 1970

Library of Congress Catalog Card Number: 70–122902
© 1970, by Herder and Herder, Inc.
Manufactured in the United States

# Contents

# Acknowledgments

I would like to thank the following persons for assisting me in writing this book: Sister Janice Futrell for helping me immeasurably by editing the manuscript and sharing ideas; Dr. Joseph Ruffin for advising me about those sections of the book concerning the psychology of change; Margaret Landis, Pauline Sumonka, and Tonya Trimble not only for contributing ideas but also for making the community that is the experiential basis for the book; and Suzanne Kelly for enlarging my thinking about various styles of religious living.

This book is dedicated to Margaret, Pauline, and Tonya in memory of Sister Mary Placida Brady.

# Introduction

MAN is a hoping creature. When we say that he is rational, we also mean that he is hopeful. Rationality enables him—indeed it causes him—to ask three questions: What can I know? What should I do? What may I plan, or hope, for the future?

Different times in history demand an emphasis on one or other question. In an age of science, "What can I know?" is paramount. In a period of moral or practical crisis, the important question becomes, "What should I do?" Currently in the world and in the Church, there is an emerging mood of expectancy and adventure; we are accenting the question, "What may I hope?"

Since we change according to what we hope, our first question regarding change must be, "What *do* we hope?" Perhaps the term which best covers the hope of all us is the scriptural one: the City of Peace. *City* has a modern ring and implies community; *peace* hearkens to faith and to ultimateness. In a way, all of us—liturgists, canonists, theologians, housewives, politicians, students, religious—are working in our streets to construct the City of Peace. For to hope as a person who is adult and Christian means not only to know what we can know and to see what we should do, but also to activate our hope to the sticking point.

Not just the pattern, but also the quality of change depends largely on the hope which inspires it. So hope should be mature and holy. It should also be realistic. Without reality, hope becomes make-believe and will effect no practicable plan for change. It is in the spirit of reality, or of realistic hope, that we will consider change in this book.

On its best behavior, change causes creative tension among persons as they move into a new order of life. Change, in this positive sense, describes one of our most profound human experiences: that of holding our present and helping to form our future.

But change is not always on good behavior. Particularly today, the very speed of external change and the consequent demand for rapid and radical internal adjustment can cause change to become a destructive rather than a creative experience for some of us. At these times, three major dangers arise.

One danger is that we can become unkind under the tension—unkind, not in the sense of passing sarcasm or defensive remarks, but in the sense of a profoundly destructive attitude by which one attacks the very personality of another. Such unkindness can cement a person in a position more quickly than conviction can. Experiments geared to test attitudinal change indicate that "aroused" subjects—that is, those angered or humiliated—reject differing positions with greater vehemence and permanence than unaroused subjects.

The second danger is that what might have been healthy tension in a normal situation can become abnormal anxiety in a stress situation. This kind of anxiety arouses associate passions: illogic, fury, hatred. In such an emotionally charged situation, balance becomes almost impossible to maintain, and those who are normally balanced may *assume* one of the extreme positions. With the ranks of the extremists thus swollen, the tension shifts from fanatics versus moderates to fanatics versus fanatics. No good resolution can come from that. No fanatic decision is ever fair.

Finally there is the added danger that we may come to believe that we cannot meet the demands of the situation, that we cannot change. To believe that and to act accordingly is to abdicate our human freedom.


Religious women may sometimes feel as if they are caught in three concentric circles of change: the world, the Church, the community. As these three life realities rapidly present new attitudes, concepts, language, customs, and rules of life, religious can begin to feel that they are in a whirlpool of change that leaves them no opportunity to re-establish balance or to redefine direction. Nothing so intensifies that helpless whirlpool feeling as does the lack of understanding about what is happening, or the sense that the momentum of change is out of one's own control.

When we feel that we are not changing according to what we hope but rather that we are toyed by some untamed force that threatens to bend or break us according to its own illogic, then change becomes a negative experience in our lives. We become unkind. We become furious and hateful. We despair.

It is imperative, therefore, that all of us first become informed about the processes and the psychology of change and then come to formulate our hopes and to execute change in our own lives. By trying to understand our own attitudes toward change and thereby control the direction of change in our lives, we can move more calmly and directly toward that for which we hope: a community that is at once religious and modern—a community in and for the City of Peace.

In my previous book, *Sisters for the World*, I considered a major basis for change: namely, that each sister is a unique female person who relates to herself, to others, and to God according to her own reality and to the reality of the times. I also outlined a plan for a new style of community living based on those two realities. The present book is a follow-up of *Sisters for the World*—not in the sense of enlarging on that plan or of suggesting another life style, but in the sense of presenting some basic concepts which spring from the reality of this time in history as well as from an experience of religious community in this time.

The first part of this book is concerned with the psychology of change, and includes insights into the creative possibilities of anxiety and good humor. In the second part of the book, we will try to apply to religious community some of those principles of change as well as some new religious insights. The ideas presented here are in no way comprehensive or complete; both the experience of community and of religion are too richly complex for a simple "guidebook." The book is meant simply to articulate a hope and to give hope a shape, a nudge toward reality.

# I

## *ELEMENTS OF CHANGE*

# CHAPTER ONE

# The Open- and the Closed-Minded Personality

Two types of people are involved in formulating hope and effecting change: the extremists or close-minded, and the moderates or open-minded. These two groups of people, confronting and resisting each other, determine the degree, the pace, and the direction of change. Variations in extreme and moderate personalities might go unnoticed until some value is questioned and seems likely to be changed. In that situation, differences become pronounced as most people join one or the other group. Each group dusts off its system of belief concerning the value in question and marches to a position on the so-called line of change, or change-line.

The change-line has a simple anatomy: a middle and two ends. A straight horizontal line describes the middle. Its two extremities are bent down and under so that they meet back-to-back. When a change situation arises, we may either flee to an end-line position or stand somewhere on the middle.

Ends are more secure. They have a wall to back up against, and that leaves only one flank to defend. The middle, however, is open. There are no walls, so one must provide his own balance, protecting himself all the while from both directions. To locate on that middle line requires such personal concern, conviction, and choice, that a person doing so might be called an "ardent moderate." There are, it is true, a number of people who do not take any position toward change, although at various times they may appear to do so. They are sometimes credited with standing in the middle, but locating there demands more stamina than the indecisive are capable of.

Some of us might want to label the two ends as "conservative" and "liberal." But that would be inaccurate. The ends are the territories of the fanatic conservatives and the fanatic liberals: the closed-minded. Both groups, thinking that they are at polarities with each other, would doubtless be discomposed to learn that philosophers and social scientists classify them together. The extremists on either end are the closed-minded as opposed to the open-minded in the middle. "Though they seem at opposite poles, fanatics of all kinds are actually crowded together," declares Eric Hoffer. "It is the fanatic and the moderate who are poles apart and never meet. The fanatics of various hues eye each other with suspicion and are ready to fly at each other's throat. But they are neighbors and almost of one family."[1] The tension of change, then, tugs not so much between end and end as between ends and the middle.

Open-minded and closed-minded persons, like any other human category, are theoretic. Even within the theoretic groups, there is possibility of infinite variety, just as many directions besides due southeast lie between due east and due south. Nevertheless, there are patterns recurrent enough to enable psychologists to draw up descriptions of general types

[1] *The True Believer* (New York, 1951), p. 81.

4

called variously closed-minded, extremist, or rigid personalities as opposed to open-minded, moderate, or flexible personalities.

The essentially closed-minded person is one who finds it extremely difficult to alter an opinion or a course of action when the alteration refers to anything he values, whereas the essentially open-minded person finds it easier to adjust attitudes and actions by enlarging or modifying value concepts. Both closed-mindedness and open-mindedness have their genesis in some unique personality disposition which has been fostered by early experience and stiffened by habit. Closed-mindedness or open-mindedness in these people is more than an attitude; it is a character, holistic and pervasive.

Since we find ourselves working with, for, or against closed-minded and open-minded persons as changes occur today in the Church and in religious community, it seems imperative that we discern something of their nature. Our purpose is not to encourage finger-pointing but to increase understanding and acceptance of ourselves and others and to clarify our own ground for change.


The difference between open- and closed-minded persons does not lie in intelligence or esthetics, in morality or holiness. Nor does it always lie in the act or in the motivation. For example, people who leave the Church or leave a religious community may be either open- or closed-minded. So may be those who remain. A closed-minded person will more frequently remain loyal to a belief system as it is and as it has been, whereas an open-minded person will "more frequently find an ingenious, creative solution that saves the system so that it is unnecessary to defect from it."[2] The closed-minded, remaining in the Church or in a community out of loyalty, aim to maintain the status quo. The open-minded, remaining also out of loyalty, hope to change the status quo through creativity.

It is in several psychological variations that the open-minded and the closed-minded differ. One of the most important distinctions resides in their various world views. Closed-minded persons demand a neat well-ordered world. If the world as it is is not in good order—and it never is—they at least hold the blueprint that can set it right. The "right" world may be designed according to an idealized past or one newly fashioned out of the shambles of the old; in either case there *is* a right world and a blueprint for it. When the world is thus well ordered, it is easy to discern good from evil, and so closed-minded persons are apt to be judgmental and to rely heavily on authority to declare and enforce good. These tendencies originate in the attitude toward parents. Closed-minded persons either idealize their parents or else see themselves as victims of wicked or weak parents. Their emotional attitude is an either/or one; rarely is it ambivalent. This "inability to express emotional ambivalence toward parents predisposes one to form an authoritarian outlook on life."[3]

Basically, the open-minded person sees the world as a friendly lived-in place. It follows that people in the world are friendly and thus generally acceptable, regardless of their be-

[2] Milton Rokeach, *The Open and Closed Mind* (New York, 1960), p. 256.
[3] *Ibid.*, p. 359.

liefs or personal weaknesses. Such an approach to life begins with a realistic and necessarily ambivalent attitude toward parents. If a person has argued with his parents, challenged some of their decisions, and even recognized that, although he loved them, he also hated or resented them sometimes, then he can be much more honest about any authority thereafter.

In adult life, extremists usually follow the patterns of their early life. Those who "respected" parents now respect authority, and those who resisted parental authority now resist religious authority. Sometimes, however, the pattern is inverted in adult life. Those whose dominating parents caused deep unconscious resentment might finally express that resentment toward the parent-figure seen in a religious superior. Or those who lacked the security of sufficient authority when they were young, now seek that security in puerile dependence on and attachment to religious authority. In any event, extreme dependence on authority or extreme resistence to it indicates closed-mindedness.

For the open-minded adult, human authority like parental authority is good. But it is not always all-good; neither is it all-knowing nor all-just. These feelings may cause uneasiness in a moderate person, but they are not an occasion for extreme anxiety. In fact, he is more relieved than disturbed by his admission of imperfect people in an imperfect world, for it relieves him of the staggering and hypocritical necessity to be always all-good.

What is true of persons in general is certainly true of religious women. Since the convent is a kind of world itself, religious can have a world view within a world view; and it is sobering to reflect that those two views probably coincide.

The world is only half the cause for a world view; the viewer is the other half. Like the world, then, the convent will appear to be either basically friendly or basically hostile. Religious who are extremists also tend toward total submission to or total rejection of religious authority. Whether she seems hostile or compliant, the closed-minded religious depends on authority. The very presence of authority provides a security which she cannot well do without. If she is miserable, it can be the fault of authority. She may meekly accept the misery as something God sees fit to impose through the superior, or she may loudly decry it; but the fact is, she is relieved that the situation is not *her* fault.

In this regard, a new threat has recently reared its head in the life of the sister who is extremely compliant. That is the increasing prevalence of collegiality. Nowadays more and more religious superiors refuse to be authoritarian; they leave most decisions up to group vote or to individual preference. The religious who would blindly accept the decree of an authority-figure finds it hard or impossible to accept that same decision made by her peers through vote. And having the responsibility of decision cast upon her is sometimes literally terrifying. She may react to this threat of freedom by denouncing the new methods, or she may withdraw her allegiance from immediate authority and intensify her allegiance to more distant authority—like Rome. But the Congregation for Religious is neither direct nor personal, and so the religious is still left in a precarious situation. Something important—the need to submit to authority—is being withdrawn, and she is left in jeopardy.

Further evidence of psychological variations in closed-minded and open-minded persons is their sense of history, or sense of time. For the former, time is fragmented into past, present, and future, while for the latter it is fluid.

Since the world they view as hostile is the present world, the extremists do not like the present. Regardless of what point in history is present to them, they dislike it as an aberration and deformity of what was good in the past or of what could be good. That dislike plus a dread of the future cause extremists to de-emphasize the present. Yet some of them cling to the present, for who can know what the future will hold?

In a way, the future is as disliked as the present. It is the most ambiguous medium in man's cognitive world. And extremists do not like ambiguity. The mystery that is future causes some of their most acute anxiety, and some of them spend all the present time planning for their safety in the future. But it continues to haunt them. Like some relentless beast, it is constantly, invariably there and threatening.

Two ways of coping with this anxiety are open for ultra-conservatives and ultraliberals. Some turn their faces to the past. If they consider the future at all, it is over the shoulder as a possible restoration of the past. Other extremists, usually the ultraliberals, want to demolish past and present and build a new future. With a show of bravado, they ignore today and propose unrealistic plans for tomorrow. The two groups together set up a kind of antiphonal chant: "Let's go back to the past and reform ourselves." And the response: "Let's abolish the past and start all over."

Meanwhile, the ardent moderates tread the middle line. They do not see time as shredded segments of past, present, and future, but rather as a continuous flow. These open-minded persons see "the present as the legitimate offspring of the past and as constantly growing and developing toward an improved future: to damage the present is to maintain the future."[4] For the open-minded, the future has its own degree and time. It can stretch into the final kingdom, or it can be the land lying directly before our feet. Thus the moderates see the soon and near in terms of the ultimate future, and so they cannot despair over any event in the present.

This sense of connection keeps the open-minded religious in touch with her heritage and encourages her to accept and to retain many traditional values. At the same time, it puts her in touch with persons yet to follow her, and so she renews those values.

For everything we really value, we have a system of belief—that entire set of ideas, habits, customs, and convictions that accrue around the same subject. We may have one, for instance, about education, another one about child-rearing, another about religion or religious life. Both open-minded and closed-minded persons hold systems of belief, but they hold them differently.

When there is a possibility of radical change occurring in a particular system of belief, we face that possibility in a partic-

[4] Hoffer, p. 70.

ular way. We can say that we take a position on the change-line. Those at one end might want sweeping change, whereas those at the other end might want no change, but both groups are extremist, or closed-minded. Each group, having created a system of belief for a particular value, believes that its scheme is inherently right.

The moderates, on the other hand, find it in themselves to be more flexible. Partly because open-mindedness is characteristic in them and partly because they cherish the value in question, they are willing to modify or expand it, to give it room for growth.

In the case of religious life, the system of belief will include notions about prayer, celibacy, piety, apostolate, friendship. In some cases, the system will even include beliefs about gestures, dress, tone of voice. The strange thing about the system of belief of a closed-minded religious is that all those elements are almost equally important or are somehow equated. Dress and celibacy might serve as examples. One extremist's sentiments toward modern dress may be: "If you're going to dress like that, you may as well get married!" Another extremist with an opposite but equally rigid arrangement of beliefs may consider dress and apostolate equally important: "I simply cannot work effectively wearing that garb."[5]

These examples point up another interesting fact about a closed system of belief: not only are all parts of the system equally important, but the whole system stands or falls with each element in it. If one element is changed, much or all of

[5] The example of dress is used here not because it is such an important part of religious renewal but because, by now, most of us have experienced this change and can therefore identify with the example.

the system must also be radically changed; even one deviation may lead—in their thinking—to disaster. Unimportant customs, then, take on a power of preservation which they do not in reality have. Such thinking may see cloister not as a custom befitting a given time and culture, but as an absolute necessity for the celibate condition. That very association was made in a recent article: "To put the matter in plain old-fashioned language, no celibate can live without a cloister and one step outside the cloister means a violation of the spirit of celibacy and, by logic and nature, a first tiny step toward marriage."[6]

It is little wonder, in the light of this kind of thinking, that a closed-minded religious can be literally thrown into panic when religious dress is changed radically. To her, that change alters *all* the elements in her system of belief about religious life: it means that celibacy is threatened; it means that poverty is abolished; it means that prayer is distracted. In short, not just one element but the entire system is affected. When this occurs in regard to something we truly value—like religious life—the consequent anxiety can become catastrophic.

In the open system of belief held by ardent moderates, however, one element can be changed without toppling the entire system and without jeopardizing the value itself. To keep the same example: dress can be changed and, if it affects other elements in the system one way or the other, it may be only that it intensifies some values. It may cause a religious to internalize and deepen her commitment to celibacy, to re-establish poverty in a modern setting, and to use to apostolic

[6] A. Durand, "Chastity Is Not Celibacy," *Sisters Today* (July 1968), p. 614. (The article is not typical of *Sisters Today*.)

advantage her greater freedom to move and mingle.

The precise change that destroys the peace of mind of one woman slightly boosts the spirits of another. One feels that the thing she values is threatened; the other feels that the value is clarified.

Since moderates can tolerate more and different ideas, it may at first seem strange that, when the two groups do change, the moderates are much slower. The gradual approach, however, is in keeping with the general characteristics of moderate persons.

Being open-minded is not synonymous with being indiscriminate. When a system of belief—or a new element within a system of belief—is presented to an open-minded person, he neither rejects it nor accepts it at once. He works through it, one point at a time. Open-minded persons refuse to have an idea "rammed down their throats"; they "genuinely feel the need to work through, to reconcile the new with the old, even if they do not have to, and even if it delays solution."[7] Moderates may not demand a world that is perfectly ordered, but neither do they want a chaotic world. They try to synthesize, to bring new ideas into play without destroying all the old ones.

Today many religious are in this process of working through new ideas and maintaining a continuity of new and old values. The process is slow, but those who are open-minded will find—and are finding—creative ways to preserve real values with new vitality. They may, for instance, work

[7] Rokeach, p. 240.

13

through a new idea about the value of poverty and modify it to a value of generosity. The original value—detachment from material wealth for the sake of others—is retained. Besides that retention, the value itself is made more positive, more modern, more realistic.

Expectedly, open-minded persons tend to hear more and to remember more accurately. Closed-minded persons, on the other hand, employ "selective" hearing and memory. It is the old notion at work that we hear what we want to hear. If a retreat master says, for example, "Sisters must update their lives but should at the same time respect their traditions and hold onto the best in them," he can be remembered by one group of extremists as having said, "Sisters *must* update their lives. Period." At the other end of the change-line, the message comes through: "Sisters must respect their traditions and *hold onto* them all. Period."

After new ideas are worked through, new ways of implementation must be found. All that takes time. Extremists do not like to take time. Closed-minded persons, if they change at all, prefer the all-at-once system. They are not apt to think out or work through. In other words, they do not try to bring an intellectual harmony between the old and the new. This is not because they are less intelligent than open-minded persons but because, in the particular belief system in question, they have over-simplified and stripped away variabilities. It follows that they will take an either/or approach to the issue.

Perhaps this approach explains the phenomenon of persons who suddenly switch from one extreme to the other without touching middle ground. For example, some religious who seem to have taken an extremely liberal viewpoint at the out-

14

set of religious renewal suddenly switch to the other extreme. On the other hand, there are religious who seem to be very strict in interpreting and abiding by religious rules and customs. One of these sisters may decide—usually quite suddenly —to leave the convent. At that point, she is likely to change her entire system of belief to accommodate her new position. Rules that, to her, once marked the way to salvation now hail the way to neurosis. Her new detestation of religious authority and religious life may extend to the Church at large, and so the once "model" sister may turn agnostic. This ironic situation is not alien to the nature of extremists.

It is hoped—for the sake of reality and kindness—that the tensions resident in the human situation have been overdrawn here. It should be re-emphasized that none of us is a *totally* open-minded or closed-minded personality. All of us have closed-minded tendencies in some areas and to some degree. If we do not think so, then perhaps we are closed-minded about being closed-minded, and that is indeed a predicament. If we count ourselves as primarily open-minded or moderate, we should then admit that we have the most variable position on the change-line. We are likely to tip toward first one extremity and then the other; none of us is constantly balanced at dead-center.

We must also remember that the open-minded may— through fear, reaction, arrogance—become more rigid; and the closed-minded may—through grace, education, determination, love—become more flexible. Change is always possible.

15

# CHAPTER TWO

# The Dynamics of Change

WHEN we say, "I have been closed-minded," we state a fact, not a destiny. Yesterday and today lean into tomorrow but do not have a stranglehold on it. If we could not change, then a study of persons involved in change would be a matter only for despair. We make it a matter for hope by hastening to add: with these insights we can change.

As a matter of fact, in one sense it is impossible *not* to change. The man, for example, who would say, "I hold the same position on birth control that I held twenty years ago" does not, by that statement, avow that he has not changed. Quite simply, his world has changed. If he has followed the birth-control debate and rethought his position, then he has changed insofar as he holds his present conviction with a difference. If he has refused to entertain any other possibilities or to listen to any other discussion, then that very refusal means that he has become more closed-minded and thus also he has changed.

One inescapable change situation which we all undergo is *anxiety*. If we first follow the process of change as it occurs in general anxiety situations, then we can more easily comprehend the pattern of more deliberate change.

If we define anxiety as a total process involving first a perception of challenge or danger and second a response to that challenge or danger, then we see that anxiety is coupled with change. The perception of the challenge causes an emotion of excitement which we call anxiety. Our response to that challenge causes an action which we call change.

We all know that this emotion can be a negative experience which sets up fear, worry, sleeplessness. In extreme cases, such anxiety can stunt our psychological growth. However, anxiety is a perfectly normal human experience and, as such, has also a positive meaning. Positive or normal anxiety is a powerhouse of creativity and a source of maturity affecting us on the level of relationships. Without anxiety we could not relate to others in love, we could not relate to ourselves in maturity, we could not relate in creativity to the world nor in holiness to God. We are never anxious about something unless it is somehow connected with these basic relationships. In this sense, anxiety is what makes us alert and excited about relationships and causes us to deepen them.

We cannot abolish anxiety. We can only roll with it or be bowled over by it. It therefore becomes imperative that we understand anxiety and take it on as a positive experience that invites positive change in us.


The first activity in the process of anxiety is the signaling of challenge or danger. Anxiety signals alert us to an approaching challenge and prepare us physiologically and psychologically to cope with it. As soon as we perceive the alert, our bodies summon up physical energy whether we need it or not, whether we want it or not. The amount of the physical energy summoned varies according to the perceived stress of the situation: speaking before a group of major superiors will ordinarily release more energy than speaking before the parish altar society. In any case, we seldom need all the vitality our bodies make available to us. Consequently, when the situation is over, we are left with surplus physical energies.

Psychic as well as physical energies are summoned in the face of an anxiety signal. This psychic activity results in a feeling of excitement, sometimes subtle and sometimes acute, depending on the situation. Just as there is usually a surplus of physical energy, there is also a surplus of psychic energy.

After the anxiety signal has alerted and prepared us bodily and emotionally to meet the challenge, we do in fact respond or act. This response is the second phase in the process of anxiety. In our response, we actually alter some relationship: relationship to ourselves, to others, to the world, or to God. The alteration can be a bettering or a worsening; there is definitely some change.

Normatively the anxiety process has one final phase: the calming of excitation. Like other human emotions, anxiety has a rhythm. It is a three-beat measure: excitation, action, calm. If we jerk it out of rhythm by omission of that third beat, then we abort a natural human process. This not only weakens the quality of our response, but also takes a body-psyche toll. If we do not discharge our unspent excitement, it keeps running—much like a car motor that idles at a fast rate. Besides the wear and tear on the body, this condition can injure the psyche. A person who sustains for a long time an above-normal level of excitement will come to think that his

19

condition is normal; his "perceptual field, psychologically considered, is considerably altered."[1] Not only will his ability to discern real danger be dulled, but he will have to find some way to burn up the constant excitement-energy and this may leave him in a chronic rage or with an abiding nervousness or in a constant state of anxiety over situations that do not merit anxiety.

When we discharge this excitement by relaxation, exercise, laughter, recreation, or hobby, we become calm and can quietly grow according to the anxiety response we made to the anxiety signal.

Perhaps the total process of anxiety will be more meaningful if we rescue it from the never-never land of abstraction and set it in a life situation.

Let us say that a young sister plans to approach a superior with a new or radical idea about religious life. As the time for her appointment with the superior nears, she becomes conscious of an excitement which she may call nervousness. She begins to imagine possible greetings that she may make or receive, to sort out possible opening remarks, to try to muster arguments for the defense if the need arises. Since the variabilities are infinite, her plan is tenuous. By considering these details, however, she chooses her essential attitude: obsequious, confident, respectful, brash, or whatever. Let us say she is firm and respectful.

If the superior listens cordially, the sister's emotion of anxiety will begin to subside. When the meeting ends, however, she still has unspent energy which makes her feel excited, so

[1] Seward Hiltner and Karl Menninger, eds., *Constructive Aspects of Anxiety* (New York, 1963), p. 147.

she takes a walk outside with a friend to whom she relates the story of the interview. The walk and the conversation restore her to relative calm.

The woman in the example interpreted an anxiety signal in a certain way, made a certain response to it, and then relaxed. The entire process altered her relationship to herself insofar as it confirmed in her a tendency to confront rather than to avoid challenge. When she freely chose to relieve the excitation remaining after her meeting with the superior, she brought her emotional life into harmony with anxiety's natural rhythm of peaks and calms. Besides bringing a new quality to her personal maturity, the event also altered her relationship to another—in this case to a superior—because she had begun a dialogue and so shared ideas.

Multiplied, this kind of incident will evolve into a pattern of response to anxiety situations which affects personal change.

Change has other and more profound dimensions, however, than that relatively passive level. On a more sophisticated plane, we can deliberately seek our own kind and degree of maturity and willfully undertake the behavior to achieve it. The anxiety pattern of signal and response applies also for this more conscious kind of change. The signal stems from suffering and insight; the response is made in will and action.

We all suffer because we all are less than mature. We vary only in the degree and in the consciousness of our common plight. We can perceive this suffering as a kind of vague dissatisfaction, a feeling that we are not living deeply enough, or it may come to us sharply in a recognition of our inadequacies. Always our perception of personal immaturity is in terms of relationship to ourselves, to others, or to God.

In terms of ourselves, even those of us who are relatively unreflective sense that we have one life only, that it is fleeting, and that we can get to the marrow of life only if we leave its perimeter and travel to its center. And even as we feel this impulse prod us toward maturity, we are simultaneously propelled by habitual and often immature attitudes and behavior. The pain of this dichotomy may be subtle or sharp, but when we become aware of it, we have received an invitation to change.

Generally, the dissatisfaction that causes us to engage deliberately in change is experienced in terms of others rather than just in terms of ourselves. We may, for example, experience the suffering of our immaturity when we first experience the pain involved in not loving someone deeply enough. Perhaps we have arrived at a plateau in a love and there balked, resisting the honesty required for achieving a new profundity in our concern for another. Or perhaps our pain in relationship with others will not concern an individual but a whole group, a segment of society. In this case we may realize, vaguely or keenly, that our life has fallen into a pattern of mediocrity, that we are not imaginatively using our talents, that we have not put our *being* in service.

Finally, we may first glimpse this particular pain of immaturity with a flash of insight into God's incredible love for us which leaves us acutely aware of our unresponsiveness to him.

In whichever relationship the suffering occurs, it will motivate us to conscious change only when we perceive it. At that point, the suffering has also become insight. We are then ready for will and action—the second phase of conscious and deliberate change.

How fortunate if our first impulse to change were in the direction of maturity. Usually, however, we simply want to change in order to assuage the pain, and so we are often tempted to retreat into immaturity. Finding reasons to avoid loving more profoundly, improving our service, or daring a more personal response to God seems easier than changing.

First we may ferret about in our past histories for reasons to resist mature behavior. Sometimes a person "likes nothing better than to be relieved of the responsibility for his present behavior by his wonderful storehouse of unconscious conflicts derived from his past failures."[2] Past histories—with domineering mothers, jealous brothers and sisters, hostile teachers, and with poverty, hunger, misdirection, failure—can deliver up appropriate excuses for most immature behavior.

Certain philosophical schools negated freedom and popularized the Past as ruler of the Present and Future. If we do not really want to change, we can subscribe to this concept of man. But it is not a Christian concept. Christ insists that we change—always according to our own unique personalities, it is true, but constantly finding new levels of maturity.

Don't let the world around you squeeze you into its own mold, but let God remold you from within, so that you may prove in practice that the plan of God for *you* is good, meets all his demands and moves toward the goal of true maturity.[3]

[2] William Glasser, *Reality Therapy* (New York, 1965), p. 55.
[3] Romans 12, 2.

Another means of retreat from pain or responsible action is that popular projection onto God that makes him a friendly second-rate psychiatrist who would rather see us sleep well than be great. "I just can't believe that God wants me to suffer," we say as we resist certain mature behavior. It may be that he does not directly will us to suffer, just as a mother does not directly will anguish for her daughter when she says, "I hope you will grow up to be a woman capable of courage and love and faith." But if the girl becomes that kind of woman, she will suffer in the process. God wants us to be finally perfect, and that costs something.

If we persuade ourselves of these various ways of alleviating pain, we may fall away from fidelity after fidelity, moving always further away from our own maturity. To abandon the freedom to help fashion ourselves causes us to drift into our identity rather than choose it. Circumstances will push, and we will yield. Our past will set up a current, and we may simply ride it through life.

Even when we exercise our freedom to choose change, we will sometimes drift simply because we have not the tolerance for the conflict that a great amount of freedom allows. When we cannot tolerate any more, we begin to think of certain actions or situations as *necessary*. "What we can't alter we don't have to worry about; so the enlargement of necessity is a measure of economy in psychic housekeeping. The more issues we have closed, the fewer we have to fret about."[4] Times do come when we really cannot tolerate freedom of choice, when we are physically or psychically tired, when we hang between

[4] Allen Wheelis, "How People Change," *Commentary*, vol. 47, no. 5 (May 1969), p. 61.

24

the pain that invites change and the will to change. Understanding this, we can be more patient with ourselves and more compassionate of others when, at a given point, we or they must say, "I can't. Not now." It takes growing in maturity to change *can't* to *will not*—or *will*. "I can't help with the tutoring program because teaching takes all my time," we may say. By using the word *can't,* we admit that we have foresaken or suspended our freedom to choose. To say, "I *will not* help with the tutoring program because I choose to devote what time and energy I have to teaching" is an entirely different statement, reflecting a choice instead of a necessity.

We need to realize that our growth in that kind of maturity will be slow and dubious, gained finally only by dogged and inventive cunning. Conviction that we *can* change must accompany this realization; then we are ready to begin deliberately to travel toward the center of our lives.


Like individuals, communities can also change. Finding themselves in an anxiety situation, they will muster energy and make response. Some will engage in more conscious and deliberate change. Communities will mix their signals and falter in their action even more than individuals will because insight will come now to one member and later to another, making it difficult for the whole group to move in unison. Nevertheless, composite membership makes a group basically extremist or basically open-minded and so causes it to respond to change situations in a particular way.

Nowadays it would be a rare community indeed that did not find itself in an anxiety situation. However one measures change and compares eras, it is obvious that social, political, religious, and economic alterations of the past few years have affected every aspect of our lives. Our art, leisure, and emotions as well as our work and social customs have been affected. Indeed, social scientists predict that—despite the gravity of crime, population expansion, air and water pollution—the greatest challenge of the next few decades will be whether our psyches can be elastic and adaptable enough to allow us to adjust to change and to incorporate it healthfully into our lives. This present situation challenges religious communities. Are they part of something passing, something charming and quaint as antique glass, and as useless? Or will they fit in, and how?

Communities that are basically extremist or closed-minded will likely misread the signals to this anxiety situation and consequently misuse their energies in unwise or ineffective response. On the one hand, liberal extremist groups can misread the question, "Where do religious communities fit into the present scheme of things?" as a verdict: "Religious communities do not fit into the present scheme of things." This interpretation of the anxiety signal leaves a rather obvious response: to go out of existence either by a series of individual departures or by an alteration of life style so impetuous and fanatical that the essentials for religion and community are dissipated. On the other hand, communities that are extremely conservative may try to close their eyes to the signals altogether or, that failing, may set about a pantomime of change. When, for example, renewal programs give priority to questions like hem lengths, hair styles, guests in the convent dining room, individual choice of recreation time, and when even the posing of such questions elicits anger, distress, and quarreling, then the anxiety situation can hardly be labeled positive.

If society ignores them, these extreme communities will die; if society attends them, it will be to ask their continued existence with radical change. And so their anxiety situation will wax. Unable to make appropriate response or to abolish the situation, such communities will sputter in a chronic state of emergency.

Open-minded groups will find the anxiety situation different even though they are in the same historical crisis as are the extremist groups. They will read the times and perceive that the world seeks with a kind of desperation a new brotherhood in humanity and some meaning in life that maintains believable relevancy through wars and computerization and space travel. Reading the times this way, the question "Where do religious communities fit into the present world scheme?" elicits a positive answer: One of the most important contributions of Christianity today is the formation of communities of persons who can live in brotherhood and faith in this age marked by discontinuity.

A mature religious community is the epitome of the Church: believers joined in faith, worship, love, and service. Nothing else matters except insofar as it is related to those absolute essentials. To the degree that this perception is clearly conscious, to that same degree the anxiety response can become a fully deliberated plan of change. Open-minded groups, re-evaluating their nature and purpose, will find that some of the questions that receive priority when purposes are fuzzy drop completely out of question when those purposes are clarified. Such communities will seek to find—and then dare to live—a new degree and quality of community. While rooted in unchanging essentials, they will overcome old structures and move beyond present logic. Each group will try to find its own pattern and pace, to mature according to its own group personality.

Once a community has noted the anxiety signal regarding its purpose in the 1970s, and has responded to it in a positive way, it can settle in a kind of calm creativity. Like individuals, communities need a balanced emotional life. Times of stress should be framed by times of stillness. If calm follows the primary response made in the large overall pattern, there will not be frenzy in the anxiety that comes with various practical applications. When a group is caught up in discovering creative ways to serve others or to witness brotherhood, it will not become overly anxious about the roll of local superiors or the length of skirts. Accidentals will be dispatched with good-humored calm, and the essentials will stand in ever greater clarity.

And so, with alertness to pain and calmness in response, open-minded communities will leave the margin of the world and move toward the center of life.

# CHAPTER THREE

# A Question of Values

To change takes more than knowledge about the processes of change and more than the conviction that we can change. We must also *want* to change.

Wanting to change is motivated by what we value—not by what we think we value or what we should value but by what we *do* value. Value here is meant not as esteem or appreciation but rather as an existential reality upon which we base our lives. Lying as it does at the very root of change, value demands close attention.

Styles of life are based on values: the life style is the *practical reality,* and the ideal which gives it shape is the *value reality*. But value realities and practical realities have a way of slipping apart with the passage of time. We may, for instance, value Christ and his work in such a way that we choose a style called religious life. Over the years, however, our life style may slip away from its informing value. We may become so engrossed in our own education, community position, job, health, and the like that those things begin to determine what we do and how we do it. Christ and his work come to figure but vaguely in directly motivating our activities. Because religious values are what set us in religious life and because we still go through the motions of that life style, we may be unaware that they have slipped away to the bottom of our consciousness.

When the slipping away of values occurs, we may be left in that deadly condition called *mediocrity*. Even more tragic, we may be left without any clear identity—for values define our person. Value definition goes beyond states of life or occupations. By the values we hold and practice, we are further defined as pious, loyal, loving, or the like. When the value stops informing or inspiring us, our life becomes insubstantial. We claim to be one thing and are another. In that case, the person whom others "see" is not the real person at all. In a sense, we are unreal. If this discrepancy between what we claim or seem to be and what we are persists for a long time and with regard to many basic values, then our reality dims, and we move through the world like shadows.

Since values are tenuous, their loss may be so subtle and gradual that we are not soon aware of it. We may first sense their lack as a vague dissatisfaction. Life may seem to be lackluster, to have lost color and intensity. If we are both honest and perceptive, we may finally grasp that what we say we are and appear to be does not jibe with what we are. With that perception, we have received an invitation to *change,* to bring our practical reality into correspondence with our value reality. But we will *want* to effect that change only if we really and intensely hold the value in question.

What is true of individuals is also true of groups. Religious communities are based on fundamental religious values, and specific customs and traditions are based on particular values. Communities, like persons, may find fundamental

30

values slipping away and less important ones becoming more important. They may find through honest scrutiny that most of their property expansion and works are motivated by the values of economy or of public esteem rather than by a lively awareness of Christ and the way his work should be accomplished in the 1970s. In that case the discrepancy between the community's practical reality and its value reality may result in a kind of schizophrenia. This state not only weakens religious impact in the world, but it also creates an unhealthy situation for community members. It is hard to be flesh and blood in a land of shadow.

Both communities and individuals within communities are at a point in history when the opportunity to test values and to bring life into correspondence with the ideal is almost irresistible. We need then to set about the serious and exciting business of sorting out what we really value, affirming those values, and living by them. To test values, we must engage in three processes: choosing, prizing, and acting.[1]

The first test of value is choice. To choose means to give thoughtful consideration to alternatives, then freely to select one.

In today's world, options seem to be multiplied; art and news media as well as our own mobility put us in touch with worlds of possibilities that yesterday we did not know existed. Bewildered by the number of options, we may be

[1] See Louis E. Raths, Merrill Harmin, *et al.*, *Values and Teaching: Working with Values in the Classroom* (Columbus, 1966), pp. 30 ff.

tempted to play roulette and call it choosing, or to leap from one possibility to another and call it deciding. The act of free and deliberate choice is not a game, however; it is a life adventure.

The adventure of choosing values is affected by the traditional obstacle of "falling into" a life style which represents a value.

Individuals can "fall into" marriage or religious life or careers. The dating-engagement-marriage sequence, for instance, can be an automatic set of events. A woman may find herself living out her years in marriage without ever having *chosen* marriage. In a sense, then, she does not *value* marriage. A woman may also "fall into" religious life. She may be a naturally pious girl from a "good Catholic family" who was simply expected to enter the convent and who did what was expected of her. Or she may be a convert to the Church, so enthusiastic about it that entering religious life is almost inevitable. Unless at some point these women *choose* religious life, they do not value it.

To choose religious life means to consider the values of marriage, motherhood, a single career in art, scholarship, or service, the direct and total involvement for God's kingdom —to consider them all, perhaps to esteem them all, and then to choose one. This process of choosing among alternatives applies both to basic life decisions and then to choices thereafter made to correspond with that basic decision. We do not choose once and for all; we choose again and again. The initial choice determines our *state* of life; the subsequent choices determine the *quality* of our life.

We may say there are "degrees" of marriage and of religious life as there are degrees of commitment to art or other secular goods. A woman, for instance, who chooses marriage and then lets it drift along is not as involved in the value of marriage as she who deepens her marriage by making choices through the years to be honest and creative in love. The first woman will never comprehend, much less experience, the *quality* of marriage that the second woman will. Likewise, the woman who becomes a religious may, in a manner of speaking, be "more" or "less" a religious. She may make choices that carry her from the periphery to the center of life, or she may make choices that in time carry her subtly farther and farther from what she set out to be.

The recurrent choices not only make our lives more or less intense. They also define us as persons. Choosing is "an act of self-definition by which the ego elaborates and shapes the reality of the structure of the self," says Gustave Weigel. "The self needs affirmation or else it withers, withdraws, becomes less and less self."[2]

Having chosen a value, we must cherish and affirm it. The second test of a value is this prizing and affirmation. If our relation to a value is purely intellectual, we cannot cherish it. To cherish means to involve the heart. Perhaps this can best be understood in terms of legal knowledge as compared with moral knowledge.

Legal knowledge tells that something must be done or avoided and tells us, too, the manner of doing or avoiding.

[2] "Theology and Freedom," in *Foundations for a Psychology of Grace,* W. W. Meissner, ed. (Glen Rock, N.J., 1966), p. 193.

A religious, for example, may know *how* to keep a vow of poverty. In a traditional community she may give an accurate inventory of all her possessions every Lent and give and receive only with permission, or in a new community she may be accurate in keeping a budget and contributing to charitable causes and to the general community fund. And doing all that, she still may not cherish the value of poverty. Legal knowledge is not enough. It takes moral knowledge to gain insight into the heart of a value. A religious with moral knowledge about poverty will see it as a kind of prodigal generosity, a happy freedom with God's gifts.

Moral and legal knowledge apply to our state of life as well as to particular values. Moral knowledge is what makes religious life—or any other life—exciting and enables us to relax in it and laugh about it even while we are intense in our commitment. Legal knowledge alone saps the adventure from a state of life, making it a duty to be fulfilled according to prescription. Surely the person with moral insight cherishes her basic life-value more than the one with only legal knowledge.

When we prize a value, we are willing to declare it even when that declaration contains a risk.

Today, for instance, we experience a certain headiness in our new freedom and image. We look different nowadays, and our talents are more public. For the time, people are a bit fascinated by the "new nun." We like the attention and the approval. When some persons or groups challenge us or question us about our values, we do not like to answer in a way that may shatter our image or result in disapproval. Integrity may be more difficult for us than we would have suspected.

In our eagerness to maintain approval, we may forego witness. It is a good test. If we really cherish religious values, we will declare them. If we do not declare them, we perhaps do not really prize them—at least, not existentially.

Perhaps that force within a value which seeks to affirm itself explains the phenomenon that so many religious today declare their vows or promises in parish churches rather than in private convent chapels. That declaration seems to say that both the individual and the community have reconsidered religious values, have perhaps deepened or altered them, and —being pleased—want to affirm them to the world.

After making a choice and affirming it, we act consistently according to it. Action is the third and final test of value. Action is what brings appearance into harmony with reality, or practice into correspondence with value.

If, for instance, we value prayer, we will not just make an intellectual and emotional choice of prayer and a declaration that prayer is good; we will also pray. If we value service to others, we will do more than promise service and wax eloquent about it; we will actually serve. If we value celibacy as a basis for religious life, we will neither be aloof nor play at romantic intrigue; we will love people profoundly and warmly as mature celibate women.

For both communities and individuals, the action that results from studying and clarifying a value and from liking it and affirming it will at times be fairly radical.

Let us say, for example, that members of a community have reconsidered the value of poverty. They may realize that there has been a discrepancy between what they have been and what they have professed to be, and they may discover that they have devised a rhetoric to explain this discrepancy —"Even though the community is wealthy, the individuals within it can be poor. At least in spirit." After admitting this variance, the members of the community may decide that poverty as such is not a value at all—not for them. They neither choose it nor cherish it nor live it. Although they disclaim *poverty* as a value for them, they gain a moral insight into the *spirit* of poverty. This introduces them into a whole new concept of generosity and justice—values they *do* choose, affirm, and wish to act by. The resulting actions will include some radical changes in life style. For instance, in order to be generous with time and talent, all rules concerning communication, travel, schedule, and apostolate have to be reconsidered and many of them altered or altogether dropped. In order to practice justice in a modern American way, rules concerning salaries and customs related to payment for medical and other services will have to be altered, and citizens' taxes paid and social security drawn.

A community will not alter its life that radically simply because its members *think* they value generosity or even because they feel they *should* value it; only if they really choose and cherish a value will they change their life in order to give that value a practical reality.

A shift from theory to actuality makes interesting reverberations in the recurrent choices we make as we live out our basic commitments. Some of us made our first choice of poverty and obedience ten, twenty, forty years ago and made subsequent choices to live out those values in particular ways. Now we find ourselves choosing very opposite ways to live out essentially the same values. A decade or so ago, we ordered our lives through permissions and kept the cloister and silence after professional work hours; now we sign our own checks and spend much time phoning, writing, traveling, and talking.

To some religious—especially the open-minded—such changes make life an adventure which carries them ever closer to their own authenticity. Based on the originally chosen values, the changes cause them to *be* now what they said then they would be. Although some open-minded women will pace themselves slower than others in regard to change, none of them will find it deeply unsettling. Change is relatively easy for them because they hold values with both firmness and flexibility. Firm because they have deliberately chosen a good from among alternative goods. Flexible because they prize the value and perceive that it can thrive only if it can change.

Other religious—particularly the ultraconservatives—will find the same change scandalous or devastating. In some cases they will be unable to bring themselves to act according to these value shifts even after the community has given an official stamp of approval to the change in question. Holding their values, as they do, with more firmness than flexibility, the closed-minded will find it painfully difficult to modify them. But it would be unfair to think that they are incapable of such change. If they are alive and loving, they can choose and cherish, and thus they can change. If they really value something, particularly Christ and his work, they will want to change. And so they will.

CHAPTER FOUR

# *The Comic Spirit*

LAUGHTER sweeps away sham, self-righteousness, outworn customs and ideas. It generates reality and humility. It imparts an unmatched quality to individual and community maturity. Without laughter, change would be labored, sometimes even cruel. With laughter, change will be easier and always good-humored, for laughter is the expression of good humor.[1]

The natural habitat of good humor and its expression, laughter, is the comic vision. Only one who believes in life after death can hold this vision which sees the full human cycle as birth-struggle-death-resurrection as opposed to the aborted birth-struggle-death cycle called tragic vision.

We think automatically of the dramatic expression of these visions in tragedy and comedy; but even in drama, tragedy holds a moment for the man with comic vision which it can never hold for one with tragic vision. At the moment of inevitable catastrophe in a tragedy, a person with tragic vision is led to think: "Life is such a bad dream that it is better not to dream at all. Non-existence is better than existence." At the same dramatic moment of disaster, a person with comic

[1] We are speaking here not of laughter that is harsh, empty, or sarcastic, but of the expression of good humor.

vision can intuit that there is a supersensible world, another kind of existence. The mind moves through suffering, moves from the blindness of inevitability to another vision of life.

If the comic vision of life alters the dramatic experience of tragedy, it certainly alters the experience of tragic happenings in life. The comic vision sees chaos as a prelude to a new world and irrational events as a transition to a higher rationality than is now known in the world. Looking at life this way is not so much filtering reality through rosy hues as it is perceiving reality-beyond-reality. Beyond the reality of chaos and scandal in the Church, for example, there is another reality: God's purifying intervention. When comic vision permits one to see reality-beyond-reality, a warm and sympathetic mood prevails which we call good humor.

Good humor enables us to be concerned with ultimates without being unconditionally concerned. Bereavement, guilt, death: these ultimates all carry tragic elements, though they are not tragedies in the final sense and of themselves. We are simultaneously fearful of them and fascinated by them. Good humor gives the edge to fascination, letting us confront these ultimates and laugh within the knowledge of good and evil. Thus Alan Paton, writing of his wife's death and burial, can say, "So do I weep over the grave, and make my song, alleluya, alleluya, alleluya."[2]

Not only does good humor help us to face guilt and death without despair, but it also relieves the negative anxiety that sometimes travels with these confrontations. We will always be anxious about them, but we do not have to be over-

[2] *For You Departed* (New York, 1969), p. 20.

anxious. When we are over-serious about guilt or death, we find it impossible to extricate ourselves from the center of our considerations. Good humor can alleviate such anxiety by giving us a kind of detachment that permits self-scrutiny. We can, as it were, step outside our normal identity or our official image and view ourselves from that outside position. The overly solemn woman who always sees herself as Sister cannot easily achieve this kind of detachment, but the good humored religious who knows that she is really Nancy Ann can occasionally and temporarily stand outside herself and shake a finger or point with laughter. Obviously these two women will consider the imminence of their own death, the weight of their inescapable freedom, and the sorrow of their own sin with different attitudes. The latter escapes neither anxiety nor the solemnity of ultimate concerns; she simply faces them with the humility and trust peculiar to good humor.

Laughter is psychosomatic rather than logical. It involves the mind, but also the body and feelings. The comic effect centers in the fact that emotional perceptions win over bald thought. When we laugh at something, our response is suffused with *feeling*. Laughter, then, expresses a kind of sensuous knowledge—which is an appropriate kind of knowledge for sensuous and thinking creatures.

Laughter is psychosomatic also insofar as it discharges energy: mental, psychic, and physical. In fact, some psychologists define laughter as a sudden overflow of surplus energy, holding that "laughter occurs only when the escape of excess energy is denied other adequate channels."[3]

If laughter can release and relieve tension within a person, it can also relieve tension between persons. People—even those at odds with one another—who laugh together, by that very action admit a common standard of truth and reality. They see the same incongruities as laughable. In a sense, they see the same reality. Reality makes a very broad base from which to resolve differences.

Humor and laughter not only help resolve differences; they also serve as antidote to suffering. The Jews and Negroes illustrate this genius for comedy in the thick of misery. When Dick Gregory jokes about sitting in the back of the bus, he is not being inappropriate. He is affirming life despite its bleak moments—or bleak centuries. As long as humor exists, there exists a will to live, to struggle, to overcome. If the absurdities of life can be mocked, they can be destroyed. Mockery cuts a situation down to size.

Harvey Cox makes a similar point in a movie review of *Alice's Restaurant:*

In recent years all of us have started to learn how laughter can save us from despair. Our emissaries of darkness, including Arlo, do an occasional handstand or somersault so we don't take them too seriously. Our laughter in the face of possible nuclear extinction (*Dr. Strangelove*), middleclass anomy (*The Graduate*) and senseless violence (*Bonnie and Clyde*) is really not heartless at all. It is the desperate man's way of insisting that all is not lost yet. Miracles still happen.[4]

[3] Marie T. Swabey, *Comic Laughter* (New Haven, 1961), p. 201.
[4] "Can We Live Together?" *The National Catholic Reporter,* vol. 6, no. 1 (October 29, 1969), p. 4.

So when we laugh with Arlo Guthrie or Dick Gregory, we join them in mocking some absurdity in life—and by that action we acknowledge a common rightness and wrongness in public life. Laughter has become social when that occurs.

If good humor relieves tension, permits objectivity, and creates intimacy, then perhaps it is most needed now in these times of change in religious communities.

Perhaps the first step in every renewal program should be two hearty laughs. First, we should laugh at our individual incongruities. After that, there could only be laughing-with, not laughing-at each other. If we can be amused at ourselves, we can hardly be grim in our judgment of another. Another laugh should be at the incongruities of the so-called "system" of religious life. Good humor about religious life is a declaration that it is good on the whole. Only that belief gives us the right to criticize it and justifies our renewal of it.

So: A sister cuts and sews a habit and two aprons in the novitiate and gets a B in Home Ec on her transcript for it. A sister sweats through five summer sessions to get a master's degree in art and spends the next decade teaching Latin. A sister practices the Divine Office so assiduously and long that she often forgets whether she is rehearsing or performing prayers. A sister has to get a white-gold watch because a less expensive yellow-gold one is against the rule of poverty. These situations—until recently fairly typical—may be deplorable, but they are nevertheless comical. By laughing at them, we mock them as absurd and so clear the way for reform.

Laughter is more than therapeutic. It is in a sense also holy, not only because it can heal and mend broken community but also because the religious spirit is the homeland of the comic view.

Both the comic spirit and the religious spirit see the paradox of good and evil. The religious spirit feels that "it is right that things should be wrong, yet it is wrong not to strive to right them"; and the comic spirit, in similar mood, "is torn between delight in the incongruities confronting it everywhere and a sense of challenge to resolve them."[5]

An unbeliever, for example, or a person with a tragic vision faces life's incongruities without humor, without delight, without a sense of play, and finally—if he looks long enough at the wrong in the world—he is led to cynicism or despair. But the believer who has a comic vision and religious spirit sets about trying to right some wrong things in a different mood. He may work arduously and decry apathy and evil but nevertheless he considers the challenge a kind of adventure and keen play, an art which shapes order out of chaos. And all the while he lives comfortably with the fact that some chaos will remain when he finishes his work.

When religious women begin creative renewal of their life style in this latter mood, they will know that no matter what they do today someone else will venture renewal in it tomorrow. For it is right that something should be wrong.

The religious/comic spirit also affects our relation to God. If we see God as the awful majesty who beckons us even

[5] Swabey, p. 240.

44

while he remains unapproachable, then no matter how solid our faith in his forgiving and loving goodness, our relationship to him cannot but be distant and formal. God is there and we are here. God is sacred; we are profane. Fittingly, then, rituals govern our correspondence with him, and restrictions govern the rituals.

The comic vision, however, minimizes that radical distance between the sacred and the profane. It allows the person in good humor to transcend order, reason, and ritual and come in trust, laughing, to God. To transcend order does not mean to despise or destroy it. Even in the mood of play, we keep the rules of the game. But we can—if we are imbued with the comic spirit—occasionally go beyond order and ritual; for "the tensions between the sacred and the profane, and the taboos enforcing them, are transcended through a momentary recapture of that state in which such categories do not exist— the state of freedom mythologically represented by the child Adam."[6]

[6] M. Conrad Hyers, "The Sacred and the Comic," *Cross Currents,* vol. xlx, no. 1 (Winter 1968/69), p. 71.

# II

## STYLES OF LIFE

# CHAPTER FIVE

# Creating a Life Style

JOHN Gardner depicted the plight of changing religious communities when he said that today's institutions are "caught in a savage cross-fire between uncritical lovers and unloving critics."[1] One can picture a religious community caught between two groups of women: those who love it as it is and defend it against change, and those who hate it as it is and wrestle to revolutionize it. One suspects that, unless help arrives in time, both defenders and attackers will help bring it down and be left looking foolishly at each other across an empty space.

We will presume, however, that there are loving critics and that religious life is not in its death struggle after all but rather struggling to become something new and modern and holy.

Those women who remain in religious life and are critical of its traditional forms must face the problem of how to bring about the new, modern, holy community. In one sense, there are as many answers as there are concerned religious. But the answers group themselves around two basic decisions: one, to help renew religious life from within the

[1] Quoted by Robert Johann, S.J., "Law, Order, and the Self-Renewing Community," *Continuum,* vol. 6, no. 3 (Autumn 1968), p. 384.

traditional structure; and two, to help create new forms outside the traditional structure.

Some advantages of the first group are that the religious will be spared the trauma of complete uprooting and that the older members will not be left alone to die out, perhaps in loneliness or bitterness or despair. There is also an advantage in the continuity that comes from working along the course that one originally set out upon. A danger is that the structure may be too old, too large, or too inflexible to stand up under the renovation of removed walls and widened windows. It may entirely collapse.

Advantages and dangers also attend the second group's decision. That the actual experience of community can be deeper since the group will be smaller and more intentional is an advantage. Also, freedom from accidentals regulated by Rome and by chapter meetings can permit more consideration of essentials regarding religious values. A danger is that the small free community can easily deteriorate into a group of career women who share the rent. The success of such groups depends on the constant intention and effort of each member —something very difficult to maintain over a period of years.

Let us discuss first renewal within a traditional community. Renewal of a large group—if it is to be an expression of the group and not an imposition by leaders—requires time and talk, a great deal of both. Some religious, the closed-minded, prefer imposition, since too much ambiguity resides in the working-through process. But the open-minded women who

freely choose to remain in their community in order to renew its life are prepared both for the educative process and
for some resistance to it. Despite the difficulties, both types of
religious must work through renewal *together,* since together
they form one community that is moving toward a new
way of life.

One part of the working-through process consists of gather-
ing and presenting facts as objectively as possible. Facts may
indicate that some changes are neither necessary nor necessarily good. If change is called for, facts can reveal *why* as well
as *that* the present situation needs altering. Without pertinent
data, we may make things different without making them
better.

Knowing and presenting facts, however, is not the same
as accepting them. Acceptance of facts—when those facts
ultimately elicit altered attitudes and new behavior—is slow
and difficult. Acceptance depends on attitude.

Attitudes are never just cognitive. They also are emotional.
Although attitudinal change is possible, it is hard; attitudes
once formed are more or less enduring. One reason for the
durability of attitudes is that they help define a person. If
one has an attitude of prejudice against Negroes, he is defined as a racist. If one has an attitude that all is right with
the world, he may be defined as an optimist. We do not
change our definitions of ourselves easily. "Specifically, when
a person's attitudes are involved in an issue, the judgment
process is no longer neutral," says Carolyn Sherif. "It is not
neutral because it relates to matters touching his cherished

relatedness, his stand, his commitment, in short the stuff of which his very self-identity is composed."[2]

As important as the facts, then, is the spirit and diplomacy in which they are presented. If it seems that our attitudes are being attacked, then we ourselves are under attack. Challenged on the level of our identity, we are less than ever apt to acknowledge the reasonableness of facts. The way we appraise a communication and its communicator affects our reaction to an idea every bit as much as the objective content of the communication does. Expressive behavior, then, should be considered an important element in the educative process.

In a group, expressive behavior can be generally classified as friendly, withdrawn, or hostile. Hostility closes off logic, and withdrawal blocks interaction. Friendliness, though, indicates to others that we like the group and that we trust them to accept us despite difference of opinion.

Friendliness cannot be faked, used merely as a persuasive "technique." It must be a feeling of genuine understanding and affection. In a group, the closed-minded person's defensiveness may paralyze friendly feelings. The anxiety that she experiences at having her values—that is, her identity— questioned consumes positive emotions. If she cannot initiate friendliness, however, she may respond to it. Therefore, the responsibility for the *spirit* of communication lies primarily with the renewers, or the open-minded. If they are courageous enough to entertain new realities, they must be noble enough to handle those realities with diplomacy. If they presume to threaten another woman by suggesting that her essential

[2] Carolyn and Muzafer Sherif, eds., *Attitude, Ego-Involvement, and Change* (New York, 1967), p. 3.

pattern of life is wrong or weak—which implies that she herself is wrong or weak—then they are obliged to reach out to her in compassion.

It would be comforting to think that gestures of friendliness would be always accepted. But that is not the case. Seeing friendly overtures as condescension feeds the fires of insecurity and the sense of humiliation for some closed-minded religious. Nevertheless, to maintain friendliness steadily and so to leave the door ajar is a duty of the open-minded. Friendliness is the non-intellectual determinant that keeps doors open, thus permitting change with dignity. No fact, no number of facts, can do that.

If, in the process of renewal within the community, religious come to a point of "experimentation," as almost every religious group has done, communication and its attendant spirit of friendliness increases in importance. Ironically, the temptation to avoid communication increases also at this point. Sometimes superiors or others judge that the upset is not worth the information. But it is. Otherwise rumors run rampant: timid religious whisper about, and aggressive ones cry out against this new and secret evil of sisters "living like seculars." If a group of religious is experimenting *for* the entire community—that is, if its purpose is to educate or to test a pattern toward which the community may evolve— then all members should be informed. That which is being done in the name of all the sisters touches the very fabric of their lives. What they have tightly woven over the years, someone is unraveling and knitting back with a dangerously loose stitch.

Open-minded religious seeking renewal within their more

or less traditional communities are apt to complain about all the responsibility that is laid upon them. Why should they be the ones always to forgive, to smile, to encourage, to overlook, to sympathize? The complaint is natural. Nevertheless, by the very fact of their open-mindedness, they have more courage than closed-minded women. When they made the decision to stay and work for renewal within their traditional group, they took on the responsibility to be patient and magnanimous.

What about the women who decide to live a religious life outside the traditional religious groups? How do they go about beginning and what kind of life style do they follow?

Like their traditional counterparts, they need much time and talk together. Since there exists no blueprint, their plan for a style of life must be created in their meeting. Each woman comes with her own ideas and variances; from the group interaction an idea emerges and takes more definite shape through more talk, modification, adjustment. Eventually the group will have a plan which is altogether its own but which does not correspond point by point with any one individual's personal or private vision. A corporate vision carries its own price as well as its own promise, and the individuals who hold it must look to the latter and not begrudge the former. Creating a life style in this manner is a strange and painful business, intensified by the fact that each woman knows that the results of the meetings are not something to be typed up in triplicate, maybe and maybe not affecting her life; the results will *be* her life.

A problem that the newly formed groups share with traditional ones is the probable presence of closed-minded women. Whereas in the traditional groups the closed-minded tend to be ultraconservative, in the new groups they tend to be ultraliberal. These women are often stirred by what we might call the "Puritan impulse." In their frustration over past conventual experience, they may be reactionary and follow a tendency to make a litany of No's to anything that smacks of religious life as it has been. No, they will not declare their intention by vow or promise. No, they will not pray in common. No, they will not share money. And so on. Such a list, of course, may be made for practical or idealistic reasons, but if it is prompted by reaction and if the group Amen's the list, they may end up having "purified" their lives of religious community altogether. Like the seventeenth-century Puritans, these modern ones will dissociate themselves from a past that holds scandal or mistakes. Also like their forerunners, they will tolerate no one in their group whose thinking or acting is at variance with their own.

In order to curb this reactionary tendency, we must try to gain an historical sense, not cutting off the past but building from it. "To cut off history," warns Rollo May, "is to sever our arterial link with humanity."[3]

Whether traditional or modern, all groups of religious women have the same tradition. They can close their eyes to it, but closing eyes has never dismissed reality. The tradition is still there—and much of it is amazingly good. Strange laws and neurotic customs mix comfortably in history with noble ideals. The strange laws are not the basic heritage, as

[3] *Psychology and the Human Dilemma* (Princeton, N.J., 1967), p. 55.

Rosemary Haughton reminds us; they are like funny or harsh relatives and, like relatives, should be acknowledged and sympathized with. God can forgive ignorance, weakness, greed; "are we so arrogant that we can refuse forgiveness?"[4]

One final point about the new religious communities concerns the kind of women involved. It stands to reason that if the group is to form an intentional community that is personal, friendly, and supportive, then each member must *intend* that kind of community and *be able* to relate positively with the other members. To achieve that degree of community demands a certain quality of maturity as well as a basic compatability. Lacking that basis, the community ideal will join many other noble ideals that have died on paper or in speech. Only living people can bring the ideal to life.

Whether a religious chooses to live out her commitment within a traditional group or outside it, one basic thing applies: the theology of religious community.

Religious life is supposed to do what the Church does, to *be* what the Church *is*. This fact should be set in bold-face on every renewal program, for it is this fact which makes sense out of the religious community. Both the Church and the religious community are—at least theoretically and ideally —organisms rather than institutions. They are composed not of laws and traditions but of Christian believers. The members are bound by love and faith, and they express that bond by communal worship. The Church and the community witness God in the world, not only by worship but also by service to

[4] *Why Be a Christian?* (New York, 1968), p. 136.

others. In both the Church and the religious community, there is a single-mindedness about the things of God that gives those things great force in the world.

But religious communities are not microcosms of the Church just in the sense of being a small-scale picture of a large canvas. Religious communities are entities in their own right, not only reflecting the Church but helping to generate and direct its spirit.

It would be exaggerated, perhaps, to claim that as religious communities go, so will go the Church. Nevertheless, it must be said that as long as there are religious communities —if they are truly religious and real communities—they will *be* the Church and will *inspire* it because that is their nature.

# CHAPTER SIX

# Celibacy: A Value for Today?

THE calm that follows a storm differs in quality from the calm preceding one. Before the storm, a few may augur danger, but most people lull in a feeling of security. Afterward, some may view the damage with a kind of despair, others with an optimistic heave ho. Most people, however, reappraise: Do we really want to rebuild this or to mend that? Reappraisal marks the post-storm calm.

Analogously we can view the storm that has recently raged about the heads of religious. Before the outbreak, novitiate numbers were swollen, and sisters were both plentiful and seemingly content. Now the eye of the storm has passed, leaving in its wake empty novitiates, dwindling numbers of professed sisters, and unrest among many of those who remain. A few religious are ready to rebuild without analysis; others see the situation as the beginning of the end of religious life. But many of those remaining are in a post-storm mood of reappraisal.

Basically, the question reads: What *are* religious women to Americans in the 1970s? Or more drastically: Should there *be* religious nowadays?

If we are closed-minded or unsure about our state of life, we will be tempted to retreat from the issue, closing our ears to the questions or claiming that we owe no one an explanation. If we are open-minded, however, we will know that we do owe an explanation of our way of life simply because of our being for others in a special way.

## Why *be* a celibate religious?

That married Christians can love God and accomplish his work with a fervor that equals or excels that of a celibate religious is obvious. A married woman with five children can pray as well as a contemplative sister. One can serve in Guatemala as a married Peace Corps member as effectively as can a missionary sister. Surely married algebra teachers are as effective as celibate algebra teachers. So are married teachers in religious education.

Yet proof of its value can be found in that celibacy is a fact, celibacy can be chosen, and celibacy is graced by tradition.

That thousands of American women today are celibate is a fact. Although it is possible that not all these women freely and responsibly chose religious celibacy or are happy in it, it is probable that many of them did so choose and are happy. Any way of life that is lived humanly and happily is a good way. That fact alone is sufficient rationale for celibacy.

That people may choose to marry or not to marry is another fact. Man has been defined as a laugher, a thinker, a ritual-maker; he has never been defined as a marrier. Thinking, laughing, and taking part in some secular or religious ritual are built into man, part of his definition. But each person has a choice of whether or not to marry. If there were no choice *not* to marry, then man could not choose *to* marry;

every man would have to marry just as he has to think or laugh.

Finally, the tradition of celibacy for the sake of religion reaches back even to pre-Church times. Most primitive peoples somehow understood that religion was of such value that it needed the attestation of virginity, either chosen or imposed. And the Church has always honored religious celibacy as a worthy way of life. Probably as long as religion endures, there will be those who want to devote themselves to it in this special way.

We can say all this in answer to the question, and our answer is right. But it is not enough. Some truth remains in the criticisms and some insufficiency in the answer.

Perhaps in the final analysis we will have to admit that religious celibacy remains a mystery, answerable only in terms of faith. But since the inquiry is made in personalistic terms, it seems fair that we try to root our answer in both faith and personal psychology. First let us consider the fact that some people tend to be celibate by reason of their personalities. Then we will discuss those who are celibate because of a value choice.

Each of us has a personal history, a unique disposition, and natural attractions. These are without copy. They are part of what it means to be a person: unique, individual, particular. We tend to follow the patterns our histories set and the promptings of our dispositions, but we are nevertheless free. Such personal realities are directive inclinations, not compulsions. They are what lead us to say, "He was not cut out to be a lawyer," or "She was always cut out to be a nurse." *To be cut out for* means *to fit by design.* We each have our own design; there are no wholesale cut-outs for human beings.

Those among us who are given to self-analysis will be conscious of the directive influences stemming from our own being, but many of us remain unaware of them.

A social worker, for example, may choose her career because she wants to help people live together more satisfactorily and because she also wants to better society on the whole. Those are her intentional reasons. Without conscious reference to them, she may also have other reasons: her disposition enables her to be both compassionate and objective, to work without the gratification of frequent notable success; something in her personal history causes her to have a particular concern for family life; maybe she is even sublimating a god-complex which needs to interfere with and rule the lives of others. All these unique personal realities may direct her—whether she is aware or not—to make a conscious choice of social work. In other words, she may be *cut out for* that kind of work, but she nevertheless also *chooses* the work.

Following our own interior pattern may lead to a level of maturity that we could not achieve in any other way. What a happy faculty we have coming from the center of our own psyches that warns us away from a style of life not suited to our particular self and that nudges us toward one that both suits us and promises our finest maturity. These natural dispositions and attractions, based on our uniqueness and personal histories, may be part of what we formerly referred to as God's will for us.

Sometimes we speak of God's will for us as if it were a

plan he has written and now holds behind his back, our business being to guess what it says. God, though, has no will for us except the publicly stated one that we move toward him in love. "This is the will of God: your sanctification." In that sense, God does not care whether we are a religious or a married woman or a single laywoman. In another sense, however, he does have a plan for us: that we be ourselves. When we follow our own pattern, we follow God's plan for us; for that secret which makes me *me* is God's uncopied, unrepeated gift—my personality. My personality causes me to respond to my history in a certain way.

Not every woman who is cut out to be single will be a religious. And not every religious will be "naturally" celibate, but she should *be able to be* celibate and able to choose a religious celibate life. Some religious resist the idea of being suited to celibacy by disposition, for they are plagued by the suspicion that such suitability is synonymous with being incapable of loving. That fear is ungrounded. As a matter of fact, people who are disposed to be single may also be disposed to love with an intensity and breadth that excels many of their married counterparts.

A highly intellectual creative personality might be less willing to serve as a really good wife and mother; she might be more suited to single life and a profession, even though her sensibilities and passions are even, sometimes, keener. Even so, she wants to be loved as a person and also to love and give.[1]

More often than not, those suited to the present new forms of religious life are so suited because of the fineness of their

[1] Eva Firkel, *Woman in the Modern World* (Chicago, 1956), p. 142.

love power and the expansiveness of their sensitivities. They are women with heart.

Whatever our natural disposition, our life style depends in the final analysis on our free election. Selection requires a number of options. The day is past when we envisioned the basic life choice in terms of a picture showing a young woman standing on a road that forked three ways, one reading Marriage, one reading Religious Life, and one reading Single Life. That usually left us with two choices, since Single Life was often thought of as a kind of refuge state for those who could not quite make either of the other two. This restricted notion of life styles cannot be blamed on the Church; she has always held—even if she did not always emphasize it—that each person could respond to God in a unique way. No, the arbitrary division of life for women was a cultural phenomenon, perhaps more popular than academic.

One result of the few options was a frequent discrepancy between what one *was* and what one *said* she was. Many religious, for example, were not religious in the existential sense. They may have chosen a life of service and an unmarried state, and the convent seemed a logical place to live out those two choices. Some of those women did not directly choose community or religion as a primary value. Often these women promptly became miserable in religious life. Their very unhappiness may testify to their honesty: something did not suit. The trappings for religious celibates simply did not fit the shoulders of these Christian women who were really secular celibates. With something out of joint in their lives, they often made the main thrust of their energy and love toward their work as teacher, hospital administrator, artist, or proctor of boarders. It was not the efficiency but the out-of-jointness that caused people to say, "Do you have to be a sister just to be a good teacher or artist?" The honest answer is, "No. Not if being a teacher or artist is the *direct and primary* value choice toward which I intentionally dedicate my life."

Nowadays these situations are less apt to occur. Both the Church and our American culture put many choices before us: marriage; career-marriage combination; single life devoted to social service; single life devoted to art; single life or married life devoted to other secular values; religious life alone; religious life lived in close community; religious life affiliated with a community. Within these many options, each of us can find a pattern that suits our person. Each of us may *be* what we say we are.

From that long list of possibilities, we are concerned here with those choices by which we commit ourselves to a particular value with an intensity that excludes marriage.

Celibacy has more to do with personal uniqueness and with value choices than with sexuality. Indeed celibacy seen only in terms of sexual abstinence probably accounts for most of the recent confusion. When we choose a value, we choose *for,* not *against.* A woman who follows her personal bents to live singly does not choose against marriage. She chooses for her own reality and, beyond that, for some particular way to live and love in the world. In following her natural and strong attraction to some secular good such as art, politics, science, social service, or scholarship, a woman may want to devote herself with a particular life-long intensity to those values— even to the exclusion of the value of marriage. She is free to do so.

To put it another way, phenomenologically the voluntary choice of celibacy for the sake of the realisation of a value is the expression of a *special sensitivity for something of deep importance in human life* which merits this total consecration.[2]

When a woman who selects a secular value as her life mode is also a Christian woman, she will bring Christian values to her secular choice. Is she not, then, a religious celibate? No. Hers is a secular celibacy, directly thrust toward some secular good.

Like secular celibacy, religious celibacy is seldom *directly* chosen. It, too, stems from a unique choice of values—in this case, religious value.

What is the religious value toward which one may direct himself totally? "The value towards which this celibacy is directed is the *Person* of Christ and his life work."[3] Both Christ and his work. So there is a mystical or personalistic incentive (Jesus) and an apostolic incentive (the work). These two are so essentially bound up with each other that they form one total motive.

[2] E. Schillebeeckx, O.P., *Celibacy* (New York, 1968), p. 85. Emphasis added.
[3] *Ibid.*, p. 87.

Married Christians and secular celibate Christians, of course, recognize the same religious value. Christ and his work are essential to them, too. But for the religious woman, these values determine the thrust of her life. To be peacemakers, to be detached, to live in a spirit of obedience—all these are commands. To everyone who would be Christian, they are necessary, not optional. Only celibacy is not a command. The *only* evangelical counsel, celibacy *for the sake of the Kingdom of God,* is the basis for religious life.

In this sense, a religious is professional. She is a "specialist" in religion and she professes to the world that religion is a value that merits one's entire life. Her talent and energy and love power and creativity are directed specifically and intensely to Christ and to the work of Christ. Religion, not celibacy, is the value. And when a religious *is* a religious in this sense, no one will wonder about her celibacy.

Today, religious may live singly or in independent or associate groups; they may be involved in politics, science, or art; they may live on farms, in high-rise apartments, or in Appalachian shanties. With increasing variety in work and life styles, the pattern of religious life has become indistinct. Nevertheless, two basic forms of life emerge: what we might call "religious life" and "religious community life."

Some religious women may choose to live alone. This was not unheard of in times past, but in modern history it is a relatively new phenomenon insofar as more women now seem to choose this style. These religious fully and consciously intend to deepen their knowledge and love of Jesus and to work for him. They may declare their intention to a bishop with or without making private vows; they may affiliate with a particular religious group by spirit and some kind and degree of sharing; or they may simply know their intentions and live by them. These women relate to the world as "sister" —that is, in a feminine way that is loving, friendly, and supportive. Perhaps their engagement in work and in a parish or worship group as well as with friends affords them a degree of community. Essentially, however, they live alone. It is a rare woman who can live thus for years, growing always in maturity and consistently resisting the pull toward the magnetic center of self. It is rare, but it is possible. These women witness a kind of womanliness the world needs.

Other religious will experience a different call from their own dispositions and unique personalities. Some internal reality signals to them that the right direction for their maturity is to engage in religious community. They want to be in touch with other persons in a daily way, to know and to be known to a degree that can be achieved only in daily living, to experience the joy and humiliation, the support and criticism that only close community gives. They want this—and they are suited for it. In community, these women share in a radically religious approach to living.

In either case, the woman who is a religious celibate has consciously chosen Christ and his work as the direct and specific value of her life.

It has not always been that religious women were religious solely because of the intensity with which they held the value of Christ and his work. And for that reason, the witness of religious has dimmed over the years, and religious life has been seriously questioned even by believers. There will always be women in religious life, of course, who are not suited to it—just as there are married women not suited to marriage and teachers not suited to teaching. But with so many avenues now open for life styles suited to various internal realities, it should happen less frequently that women will become religious for any reason other than religious value. That means there will probably be fewer religious in the future. But they will be more *religious*. The witness that has dimmed will become then bright in this present history. Religious women will be a sign—not theoretically or theologically, but really.

A woman does not become a religious in order to be a sign. She becomes a religious because she values religion. To be a sign is a result. Each religious woman is a sign that Jesus Christ is a reality—at least to her—in America in the 1970's, and that this Christ is loving and lovable. She is a sign, also, of the Kingdom, not the *way* but the *fact* that it will be. She —at least she—believes in that Kingdom so strongly that she gladly chooses to spend her life working for it, even to the exclusion of certain other values. The fact that she is celibate in order to devote herself to these religious values makes even her celibacy a sign.

# CHAPTER SEVEN

# Prayer: Ritual and/or Belief

Reality is not flat, like words on paper. Reality is time, space, people, emotions. In a sense, it is four-dimensional. To remain always a child before a reality means to view it always from the same position—usually unquestioning. To grow beyond childhood means to move around and about a truth, to perceive it from various angles. Sometimes when we shift our position in relation to a reality, the reality blurs until we settle and refocus. Then we realize that we are not seeing what we saw before. When this happens, we can become confused and begin to mistrust not our vision but the reality itself.

Our experience of prayer, for instance, differs in us as we move from childhood to adolescence, from adolescence to adulthood, and then on to more refined stages of adulthood. Besides those personal shifts, there exists nowadays the added phenomenon of communal change. It is interesting that, despite all the variations in new and re-newed communities, one thing that all groups seem to retain is some kind of group prayer. This fact attests that religious are indeed motivated by that first part of the motivating religious value: the Person of Christ. They have retained prayer, but they have not yet found a satisfactory new mode for it. With the alteration of styles of living and modification of values, communities in evitably find their earlier experience of group prayer inadequate. In the gap between old ways and prayer and undiscovered modern ways, the whole notion of prayer blurs. We do not "see" prayer the way we used to.

Perhaps this blur accounts for the awkwardness that presently attends prayer and that permeates discussion about prayer. Many of us find the Divine Office too formal for today's shape of prayer. We press for more spontaneity, personal dialogue, relevance, leisure; we seek a new ritual that is at once modern and holy. But our past experience rules against us. In the past, even so-called community prayer did not involve us in community—that is, with another person. And so we find it embarrassing to look at one another now, to talk together with God, to put ourselves, our work, hopes, faith, doubts out there before God and each other.

Even when we are not embarrassed by prayer, we are perplexed. When we form a new community life, should we wait until we have reached a point of knowledge and trust and appreciation of each other before we begin praying together? Should we pray regularly, or is it better for prayer to be a celebration of special times? What shall we *do* for prayers? Is the Eucharist prayer enough? Attempts to answer these questions sometimes lead to one or several prayer substitutes: discussion clubs, sensitivity sessions, parties.

Questions and answers alike illustrate something of the new shape that faith has taken, and point up some new and valid insights that religious have about prayer. The religious experience may be distinct from secular experience, but it does not follow that it is separate. Discussion and sensitivity and celebration should, therefore, be part of prayer experience—which is not to say that any one of them can *be* the prayer experience. Americans find it difficult to be open, even just to confront themselves. Yet communal prayer depends on some degree of openness. Surely this native difficulty is every bit as much at the root of our embarrassment as is our past habit of collective prayer in which there was no person-to-person revelation. If sensitivity sessions have tested ways to help us learn to communicate with easy openness, then those ways can be employed by persons serious about community prayer.

Theological or religious discussions, too, are a means to prayer and a part of prayer. They help us to know God better and to know how our friends know him. Ideally such religious discussion leads us to address God quite simply. Karl Rahner has perhaps given us his greatest contribution when he gave us his book of personal prayer. We cannot make his prayer our own any more than we can memorize a play script and recite it for our own conversation, but we can see how he and men like him move from wrestling with the intricacies of developing theological doctrine to conversing simply with God.

The total prayer experience, then, may include practice in openness and conversation. It may also include conviviality, laughter, and song. The point to remember—a point easily ignored—is that these techniques abet prayer; they do not make it. None of them singly should be made to assume the whole role of prayer.


Before we can discuss a new shape of prayer, we need to understand the new shape of faith. If prayer is communication

73

with God, we need to know God. More fundamental than ritual is faith. Before we ask, then, "How shall we pray?" we must ask, "What do we believe? What do we think of God?"

These questions do not threaten heresy or apostasy. They simply show that salvation is ongoing history, history with a present and future as well as past. History is "the uniqueness of a single event already present in its unchanging essence, yet constantly seeking its identity because only in this way can it renew and fulfill itself."[1] When this "single event" is God, faith has to find a new form for each person and every age. Others in other times have asked, "What do I think of God?" and have answered the question; but that is not sufficient for *us* in *this* time. We must ask the question again and today. We must find a new form of faith now in our changing, changeless God.

In seeking this new form of faith we need to examine the fabric of contemporary thought. There we find four distinct ideals: man seeks sincere brotherhood, he questions values, he admires simplicity, and he yearns for the ultimate experience. These four features describe today's man and so describe also today's form of faith. Faith is brotherly, doubting, simple, and transcendent.[2]

Faith is brotherly. Christians believe that God has called all men to his Kingdom. Christians have always believed that, but modernity has brought a new quality of brotherliness and openness that suits the enlivened social conscience of man.

Faith is doubting. The Church has always taught that faith does not exclude doubt, but many of us never quite accepted

[1] Karl Rahner, S.J., *Belief Today* (New York, 1967), p. 49.
[2] See *ibid.* for fuller discussion of these four ideals.

that teaching. Doubt in matters of faith leaves us frightened and ashamed, and we have resisted it. In the climate of honesty and questioning today, however, Christians accept doubt, they openly question the meaning of things like resurrection, they admit that faith is a risk. Paradoxically, this modern confrontation of danger causes faith to take a far deeper level in our being. Faith becomes *faith,* not apologetics or dogma. Man experiences the mystery of God in a way more profound than he could in undeviating certainty.

Faith is simple. Today's man protests structures, bureaucracies, complex "arrangements" of humans. He mistrusts fancy words and idealism that is not applicable to the human situation. He wants direct and personal involvement—in short, he seeks community. For the Christian, this means minimizing the value of paternal or hierarchical authority in preference to collegiality. More than that, it means cutting through theological data and trying to discover—and experience—a personal God who loves and forgives.

Faith is transcendent. In drugs, eroticism, in rock music and new poetry, in Zen Buddhism and yoga—in these and in other ways, today's man seeks the ultimate experience. He wants to be free, to transcend the world, to transcend even himself. Christians, enlivening their belief that God is the transcendent reality, seek this experience in religion. Liturgy and ritual become newly important as does deeply personal prayer. As we move in this direction, we come to the realization that, though the world is aging, God is eternally young; he transcends time. There is no risk that he will come too late. Transcendent faith does not do away with concern, but it abolishes frenzy.

What does this old/new shape of faith in God mean in terms of prayer?

The fact that faith is simple and personal means that prayer clarifies our identity and puts us in love-relation with God; brotherliness in faith means that prayer becomes expansive and creates community; questioning in faith fills our prayer with humility; belief in God's transcendence encourages us to pray with greater perspective and leisure.

Prayer is conversation with God. God started the conversation by causing my existence. Parents may have wanted a baby; God wanted "me." He opened the conversation with me by saying, "Be." "Surely the one thing which man finds immediately comprehensible is that the absolute mystery of God is the foundation of his own existence and that the easiest and at once the most difficult existential act is the acceptance of this ineffably loving and forgiving presence," says Karl Rahner. "This is the essence of Christianity."[3] No matter what I seem to others, no matter what my self-image, I am who I am, and God constantly loves and forgives that real me. When I talk with God, I can therefore be personal, even familiar.

Because God also loves others and so makes us brothers, prayer becomes expansive. Prayer-conversation may be between God and me, but the conversation does not necessarily center about God and me. If migrant workers strike, I may talk to God about these brothers—and he may speak to me about them. If I pray about the women in my own religious

[3] Ibid., p. 75.

community, I am inclined to expand the prayer to include all women attempting to create and sustain a new form of religious life. In this way, we can bring ourselves closer to others through prayer.

Prayer is communal in another way, too, insofar as it not only expresses community but also intensifies it.

People gather to pray, at least ideally, because they already are in community with one another and want to express the faith that is its basis. In that way, prayer testifies a reality. When during prayer we speak to God from our own honesty —not as we may seem to be but as we are—then those who are with us in prayer glimpse some deep truth that they could never know any other way. We may, for example, be plagued by doubt and may make an honest plea in group prayer: "I want to believe." The appeal is not made to our friends but with our friends to God. We cannot come away from such experience without a keener and more sympathetic understanding of each other. That is when prayer becomes a community-making event. Serious Christians are coming to realize more and more this difference between discussing a religious stance and sharing one. Sharing prayer can move us only in the direction of love.

Faith today is conscious of risk, and that consciousness declares itself publicly in group prayer. We may be jolted occasionally into noting the possibility that we are fools, that we send our voices out into Nothingness. We may doubt that God really asks us to call him "Father" and that his love for any one of us shatters all the degrees of human love we have known. At those times—and for most Americans today, those times do come—we can nevertheless gather to pray even if the only prayer we can offer at the time is a primitive heart. Courage to believe will come from the community. Ultimately, faith is an individual and highly personal phenomenon, but we must remember that it is always born in a community. It may also be reborn there.

Finally, we look to God for what is called the ultimate experience. Today has witnessed a twin movement: toward God in the world and toward him beyond the world. Modern man bears a sensitive social conscience, one that involves him emotionally and actively with men who suffer. At the same time, he has responded with new enthusiasm to the ancient pull toward God, seeking a new intimacy with him. This twin movement has nothing to do with this-world versus the next-world tension. Rather, it signifies that there is one sphere of reality, not two, in which we are totally Christian. To seek from religion a motivation for social justice without also seeking intimacy with God is to behead a single religious reality.

These observations about the influence of today's faith on today's prayer may help illumine the content of prayer, but they do not clarify the ritual.

The word *ritual* may conjure up two unpleasant notions. On the one hand, we may recall a set of motions and body actions which were fixed in some long-ago time and which have since become empty of the reality they were meant to contain. On the other hand, the word may create a picture of today's self-conscious efforts to make liturgy more meaningful by including pop and rock and folk music and art, dance,

dialogue, meals, and various sound and visual media with
the result that each liturgy becomes a spectacular that cannot
be sustained. Many people have the uneasy feeling, when they
consider ritual in this way, that the price has been paid but
services have not been rendered; tradition has been given
over, but that mercurial thing called meaningfulness has not
been won.

These notions refer not only to the liturgy of the Eucharist
but also to religious group prayer. Pews are gone, chapels are
unused, genuflections and bows are out, plain chant is unheard
—all this at least in many groups. Services employing those
elements may have been solemnly beautiful, but many religious
today maintain that they were "religious services," seldom
"religious experiences." Yet we are finding it difficult to arrive
at a new form. Obviously, we cannot create a new ritual each
time we pray together. Just as obviously, we need some ritual.

Ritual is a psychological need for man. Indeed one of
several simplistic definitions of man says that he is a ritual-
making creature.[4] We need ritual for two reasons: it is a
means of coming into contact with a value reality, and it
provides a framework for free response. Prayer ritual puts us
in touch with the value reality, God, and lets us respond to
him.

If we had always to create new rituals, then we would become so engrossed in the ritual itself that it would interfere
with prayer rather than encourage it. Ritual that is too complex and too self-conscious sidesteps its purpose and leads
again to that old grievance of substituting performance for

[4] William A. Osborne, "Religious and Ecclesiastical Reform," *Insight* (Summer 1968), p. 4.

reality, service for experience. Since man cannot always create new ritual, he tends to stabilize one. And because ritual that is too complex becomes a distraction, he periodically purifies and simplifies it.

Ideally, then, ritual combines simplicity with symbol, and stability with flexibility. When we are at home in a ritual, we can give ourselves over to the reality it expresses. Even when our feeling is at low ebb, the framework is there and allows us to participate without strain according to our current will and feeling. And if the ritual is also flexible, we can be creative in it, give it a particular shape to express a particular insight, feeling, or situation.

What holds for ritual in general holds also for that specific way in which we pray in community. In ideal group prayer, there are three basic realities: conversation with God, celebration, and community with one another. Those three essentials give shape to the ritual.

Simply put, prayer is conversation with God—and so part of each ritual should be direct address to him. Sometimes we come together prayerfully to glean insights about our work, ourselves, and social issues; such times may buoy us up, inspire us, enable us to solve personal and interpersonal problems. But we turn prayer into a kind of group therapy at best and at worst make ourselves each other's gods unless we move beyond our own conversation to talk with God.

Another seemingly "natural" part of prayer ritual is Scripture reading. If in fact, as well as in theory, we are religious because we directly and especially choose religious values —Jesus Christ and his work—then we will want to deepen our loving knowledge of God. We may bring scholarship to the Scriptures, but in group prayer we will be primarily motivated as a person eager to learn more about a Person we love. And we will also be eager to hear what *he* has to say in the conversation.

Since conversation entails listening, we need also to be occasionally silent in prayer. Being still is difficult for us moderns; being still *together* is yet more difficult. But as prayer becomes a relational experience, we may find the periods of silence longer and more comfortable.

Joining voices seems to be another important part of a community prayer ritual. Voices united say that we pray and celebrate together. Because of the festive spirit often found in real prayer, voices are usually joined in something appropriately choral and beautiful, as in song, psalm, or poetry.

Contemporary reading also holds a definite place in prayer. We live in this world, and the insights and facts about it put us in touch with the work we do with God in this world.

These elements—oral prayer, Scripture reading, silence, joined voices, song or movement, contemporary readings— these may be part of a more or less stable ritual.

As trust and loving knowledge deepen, prayer together will become less self-conscious and much more natural. Then we will be able to pray with more spontaneity in groups of two or three, not always needing the support of routine: set time and set rite. Then we will experience community in what we have perhaps prophetically called "community prayer."

# CHAPTER EIGHT

# *Witness through Service* and *Salary*

WORK usually bears two results: income and service. We talk a great deal about service but often think that the subject of income lies outside the pale of religious or idealistic consideration. Money, however, is a modern reality. More than that, it is a kind of testimony.

We are beginning to sense that in modern industrial America, money is the "natural" symbol. Grapes and grain were once the "natural" symbols, not just because they grew out of the ground, but also because agricultural people used them in exchange for services or gave them as tokens of friendship or of values. For the same reasons, sheep or oxen were natural symbols for shepherds. Most of us neither have nor exchange grain or sheep. Money is what we earn, what we exchange for goods and services, and what we give as a sign of what we value.

In a sense, we publicly declare our values by the way we make money and by the way we spend it. A woman who teaches in a school specially designed for hard-to-handle students because salaries in those schools are higher than they are in other schools testifies to a different value from the woman who teaches there in order to give a particular service. Though engaged in the same work, they present themselves to the world in two very different ways, the difference lying in the rank of values—not just in how the money is made but why it is made that way.

If money is one of the major symbols by which we present ourselves to the world, our use of it is part of our witness. We may save it for the proverbial rainy day or spend it for education or for entertainment; we may spend all of it for ourselves or much of it for others; we may be prodigal or thrifty or downright tightfisted. Because each of us is unique, we each will vary in our witness to the world. Nevertheless, some degree and kind of generosity and of loving service will be shown by any woman who is truly religious.

If money stands as one of the symbols of our person, then we need some freedom with this modern, natural symbol. Such expression, a new experience for religious today, began a few decades ago when, becoming more professional through education and experience, we began to lament our unprofessional status as "cheap labor" in the Church. A pittance was earned for what lay counterparts did for two to eight times as much, and salaries were usually sent directly to the motherhouse or superior. Women resenting this system took up the cry "Professional!" They were not necessarily puffed up with the artificial importance conferred by a degree, nor were they greedy for money; many simply realized—consciously or unconsciously—that money as a symbol was saying, "You are taken for granted." Now that we contract for the jobs we choose, our services are not so much taken for granted. It would be sad, therefore, if we remained more concerned with what money says about us than with what we say with money.

Just as the individual religious testifies something about the kind of person she is by how she earns and spends money, in the same measure each community shows what it values. Largely because of active generosity, many new and renewed communities pool salaries or living expenses. If a few full salaries are sufficient for practical living, then some religious can serve for less than full salaries. Through this variation in earning power, the community is able to expand its notion of generosity to include those things that we are often most chary of—time and talent, personality and energy. Although some in the community may end up working as hard for as little as under the so-called "cheap labor" regime, the situation is profoundly different. Now *we* say something with money: "I exchange the right to a full salary for the greater right to serve those who cannot 'afford' this service." Paradoxically, it seems that the important thing is to be able to say that money is not all that important, that its significance lies in the values it points to. That may well be a very essential witness to give in the world.

In sharing finances, we also present another value to the world: a community of people who trust one another. We value the chance to give and to receive faith, inspiration, and gladness from each other; and we testify to that by giving and receiving today's natural symbol, money. One of the first and undeniable indications that trust is weakening in any community—religious or otherwise—is a tension caused by holding back money, misrepresenting expenditures, or comparing contributions. Thus a religious who contributes four hundred dollars a month to the general funds may observe the plate of one who contributes only fifty dollars and think, "She's eating *my* porkchop." If financial tensions persist seriously and long, then the sharing system will break down and the world will see a broken community. As long as real community endures, however, the system will succeed and will be a witness to trust.

So money is not outside religious consideration at all. It can be a testimony that the goods of the world are gifts to be used in generosity. It is also a testimony that people—people we work for and people we live with—are more important than money.


Service is another witness and another fruit of work. As religious we intend to serve. Intention alone cannot be the medium of our work. We serve in reality—that is, in a particular situation wherein we meet people and work with and for them. Two major considerations guide us in this aspect of work: one, that the work be suited to our own temperaments and capabilities, and two, that the work itself help bring about God's Kingdom.

Being realistic about our suitability for a job has become our own responsibility. Less and less frequently do superiors appoint us to jobs without regard for our talents and temperaments. Nowadays superiors are more apt to approve than to appoint—if indeed we have superiors at all.

As we assume that responsibility and change other elements in our life style, it is not surprising that we are tempted also to change our work. Change is in the air. We not only look different but are also looked at differently. Caught up in this heady newness, many of us may seek different work. Work, after all, takes up most of our waking hours; it begins to seem imperative that, if we are really going to be different, we change the way we spend those work hours.

In some cases, we are justified in shifting to new jobs. It goes without saying that not all of us who entered teaching or nursing communities were "cut out" to be teachers or nurses. In many cases, however, we may delude ourselves in changing jobs, thinking that that external difference will alter our internal reality or will sharpen our witness. But work expresses internal reality more than it creates it, and witness depends more on the worker than on the work. Stradivarius's violin may be capable of producing the finest music, but that capability will be realized only if a fine musician plays it. Likewise, preaching or catechizing may be among the works most directly concerned with fostering religious values, or work among the poor may be one of the most dramatic ways to carry on God's work, but unless a person with Chrysostom- or Bosco-like talents is involved, the work may be unsuccessful. It may even be a fiasco.

With the advent of more freedom concerning the choice of work, therefore, there comes also the demand for a finer quality of maturity. We must strive to judge objectively where we are best qualified to serve. The academic judgment is relatively simple; the emotional one is not always so. If we are not prepared emotionally for a particular job, then no matter what our attraction or talent, we should not engage in it. How difficult it is, however, for some of us to judge our own emotionality. No work exists, of course, that does not make emotional demands on persons; but if the work causes us to be *constantly* touchy, sleepless, and anxious, then our choice was ill made. In such a case, we may become so involved in trying to cope with our own frayed feelings that the material of the work as well as positive religious values are diminished or lost sight of.

An added consideration for the religious woman who is also a member of a community concerns the effect her work choice has on the other religious with whom she shares community life. A job, for example, that for an indefinite number of years demands a schedule of extensive travel or of day-sleeping and night-working is a job that necessarily curtails the time spent with community members. If close community depends essentially on prayer together, exchange of ideals, and mutual support—all of which take some degree of daily living together—then that particular job is incompatible with that particular degree of community.

There was a time when a religious could remain legally in community even when—for years on end—she was not involved existentially in it. Obedience through appointment resolved the dichotomy then. But now we are in a position that requires us to make and declare a choice. In the case of a service which interferes with close community living, we can choose to live as a single religious or as a religious loosely affiliated with a group, and thus devote ourselves primarily to the service, or we can choose to change the work. Any of the options is good; the important thing is that we *be* what we *say* we are in terms of community and in terms of work. Never before has it been so easy to be honest in this regard.

If we are thus wise in our judgment of the suitability of the work both for our own personalities and for our communities, we will more easily bring a religious quality to our work. That quality is what makes our service effective for God's Kingdom.

Quality here refers not to efficiency, but to an existential and spiritual reality, to the reality emanating from the person rather than from the job. Almost indefinable, quality in this sense is nevertheless one of the most subtle and profound characteristics in all human experience. It pervades and colors actions and can even alter the nature of an action. Laughter, for example, can range qualitatively from sadistic cruelty to ecstatic love, touching all points between those extremes. Yet it is the same somatic human action. The internal reality of the person laughing determines the quality of the act.

Quality differences may also exist between good and good, making neither of them superior to the other but making each of them different from the other. Laughter, to continue with the same example, can be an act of shared delight, an act of sympathy, or an act of mutual insight which notes the same incongruities. Each of these experiences of laughter is good; one is not superior to the other two. Yet each one is different in quality.

Such quality differences are what we must try to comprehend and to trust in terms of the work of religious. For instance, social work seems intrinsically suited to religious values. The social worker meets the poor or unfortunate and tries to heal, direct, and encourage. This kind of work can be an obvious continuation of what Jesus did on earth. But engaging in social work is not *in itself* an expression of religious value. Like laughter or any other human action, its quality depends on the person and the motivation.

If we are religious because we have freely and deliberately chosen to direct our whole personalities to Christ and to his work—the Kingdom of God here and now—then our work will have a religious quality. It will witness to both the motivation and the faith behind the motivation. If we are religious for any other reason—or if our religious commitment has paled—our work will also witness to that. It is that simple. And that sobering.

A really religious motivation lets us devote ourselves not *to* our work, but *in* it to the world.

To shift our emphasis from a religious value or any other human value to the job itself is tragic, for "to be tied to the process of work may be ultimately due to the inner impoverishment of the individual"; it is a sign that "his life has shrunk inwardly, and contracted, with the result that he can no longer even conceive of such a thing [as value]."[1]

Religious community, with the give-and-take of encouragement, challenge, inspiration, and support, helps us to avoid this kind of contraction of soul and dilution of religious values. So does prayer, for in prayer we can address God about his work. When we can relate to God so personally that we see our work as his, we will never be frenetic about it. We are not god; only God is God. Ultimately, it is his job. Faith, with its attendant comic vision of life, lets us see and say that.

No amount of humor or trust will cancel anxiety in work, but both humor and trust can alter the way we experience anxiety and what we do about it.

The anxiety cycle—excitation, action, and calm—can seldom

[1] Josef Pieper, *Leisure. The Basis of Culture* (New York, 1963), p. 50.

complete itself in work. At work we are excited or moved by a situation: by a student wrestling to bring a new social concept into harmony with his own experience of reality, or by a jobless man seeking a house for his family. At work we try to respond to these situations: finding the right time to say the right word to the student, or calling a housing authority or locating a job for the man. In an ordinary work day, numerous similar situations arise which call up from us a feeling and a response. Feeling and response are only two parts of a three-part process. Rarely does work provide an opportunity for us to move completely into that final step—calm.

We therefore need a work-leisure rhythm to set a balance in our lives. A rhythm is marked by periodicity. One does not discharge all excess anxiety and arrive at deep psychic calm by cramming two weeks a year full of fast travel, or even full of sleep. Anxiety is experienced daily; some degree of calm should also be experienced daily. Periodicity itself sets up a calm; one can come to depend on her own rhythm to harmonize the feelings and the activities of her life. Praying can be one kind of periodic calm. It can even be a leisure experience at times. Being perfectly still can be another. Walking, reading, laughing, making things—each of these activities can also recreate us in calm.

*Quality,* then, depends on the intensity of our dedication to religious value and expresses itself not only in hard work but also in good humor, trust, and calmness. It is thus that we work for and in God's Kingdom.

# CHAPTER NINE

# The Communal Quality of Everyday Life

What we might call the "dailiness" of daily life is so untenable and indefinable that writing about it may seem callous on the one hand and presumptuous on the other. But dailiness should be discussed, for community is made from it. The design and the inspiration for community comes from common ideal and prayer, but the relation itself, that dynamic something that exists between and among people, is woven in more subtle ways. Dailiness includes all the subtleties of spoken and unspoken communication as well as the complications of decision making. Often a sticky, mystifying stuff, it is essential for community and maturity.

*Community* and *maturity:* these words represent goods in the life of any human being. But when they translate themselves from words or ideals into the nitty-gritty events in the quotidian of life, we are apt to shy away from them. We are much like overweight women who, aspiring after trim figures, collect diet plans, read successful before-and-after stories, and study exercise programs, only to balk when it comes to sitting at the dinner table with cottage cheese or doing fifty sit-ups every day. The push-pull tendency in us all makes us approach and withdraw from goods, embrace them in theory but resist them in practice. It accounts for the fact that the hopes for deep communion that most people have at the outset of marriages are followed by the sad report of social scientists that enduring and profound married communion is very rare indeed. So too in religious life. Idealistic women joining a new-spirited religious group heartily desire to enter into a community that will release their ego-imprisoned "I" and make them whole women. The concept of being a whole woman is dramatic; but *becoming* one is an uneven, often boring, sometimes humiliating process.

Without this process, however, one will likely live out her only earthly life without ever being known. Unknown by another human being, she will be unknown even to herself. To be without community is to hover above the stream of life. Dipping down for temporary landings does not establish us in life, but leaves us still undefined. No, at some point we must, with full deliberation, commit and root ourselves in some particular community—family life, service, or religious life. Then we are established in humanity, our lives touching others, touching also the past and the future that flows only in the stream of life. There in that community, and only there, will we grow in our own person; for no such growth occurs outside communion with others. "The unit of the human is not the solitary 'I'—it is the 'we.' Man is essentially a community, his life is a communal affair, he exists only where a plurality of individuals is in communication with one another, and shares a common life."[1]


We involve ourselves in community by means of communion, or communication. Communication consists of all exchanges

[1] Robert O. Johann, S.J., "Law, Order, and the Self-Renewing Community," *Continuum,* vol. 6, no. 3 (Autumn 1968), p. 380.

of feeling, attitude, and thought, including not only those of which we are fully conscious but perhaps more importantly those of which we are only obscurely aware. Communication's modes are many, ranging from clear verbal or physical expression to subtle non-verbal expressions.

Subtleties are like a dramatic sound track in our lives—playing always in the background, they set the mood, heighten the excitation, establish calm; they perpetually shift to capture every variation of communication. Although subtleties are difficult to pinpoint, they need to be recognized and heeded for their uncanny power in building or breaking relationships. The way we hold our mouths, lift our eyebrows, allow barely perceptible inflections in our voices: such things create bonds or barriers between people. They can convey hostility or guardedness, affection or interest. When a community is based largely on compatibility—as real community always is —we must be aware of the tenuous energy of such non-verbal communication.

Simply living in proximity with others is another kind of non-verbal communication. When we are close to someone, we feel called upon to compare ourselves with him or her, and the difference that exists can then be conceived like a latent criticism of the way we are. If a religious who is easygoing, for instance, lives in proximity with one who is in perpetual motion, each may feel reprimanded by the other, one feeling guilty because she is not sufficiently involved, and the other feeling guilty because she is not capable of a meditative approach to life. Non-verbal communication of this kind, called by Freud the "narcissism of small differences,"[2] can cause

2 Rokeach, p. 301.

resentment that, like the message itself, continues to have influence below the level of consciousness. By becoming aware of these situations, we can change them from occasions of resentment to occasions of sharing in the particular goodness of another.

In real community, however, we share in more than the goodnesses of each other; we also share in the weaknesses. We seldom make a declaration that we are lazy, quick tempered, moody, insecure; we learn and communicate these facts nonverbally. Worse than knowing that these traits exist in ourselves and in others is knowing that they will likely persist. "There are few things so conducive to despair as seeing the recurrence of weaknesses in those close to you; it enables you to read the future."[3]

From our weakness we may reach out to others for help. We may also extend help. But our essential communal task in regard to another is to accept the person and to avoid concentrating on her weakness lest we equate her with it. The good and the evil in all of us is impossible to separate. We must learn to let our evil be known and accepted, and our good be known and loved.

Verbal communication is more manageable material for making community.

There is a story, one would hope fictitious, of a man who said to his bride at the end of their honeymoon: "Now, Marsha, I love you and that's why I married you, so there's no use discussing it any more." If he never discussed it again, it is

[3] Thornton Wilder, *The Eighth Day* (New York, 1967), p. 47.

likely that non-verbal communication alone failed to carry the message consistently and satisfactorily through the decades. Words may be raw and clumsy material, but they are man's unique tool for communicating with others. And they carry their own kind of subtlety.

For an example, let us consider a group of women who gather to begin a new religious community. They argue, negotiate, dialogue, banter, philosophize—and out of the words an idea is effected in the imagination of each person. Because each person is different from the others, however, her idea will also be somewhat different. Therefore, they cannot conclude the session by saying: "Now we have discussed it thoroughly, once and for all; there's no need to refer to it again."

Ideals have a way of sinking into non-existence if they are not kept conscious. To make community, it is necessary sometimes to talk about community. These sessions need not be frequent, but they should occur.

Expectedly, the times when they are most needed are the times when we would rather avoid them. Community crises usually involve community personalities. The general question, "What about prayer?" must become, "What about *our* prayer?"—and that involves those who pray. When these questions become critical or tense, discussion becomes confrontation and can be very difficult. Unless we can engage in the discussion without anger, it can be a time of hurting without healing and so can weaken community. At these points we are tempted to rationalize: "I dislike 'scenes'." Or: "I prefer a broken or weakened community to one that is mortally wounded." In the end, we may completely avoid the confrontation. If we do, we create a sadly ironic situation; for when we reformed a traditional life style, it was surely in part because that life style provided little chance for existential community. We will not create communities without weaknesses, but how wretched it will be if we set yesterday's weaknesses in today's communities.

As a case in point, let us return to the example of the active religious and the meditative one. In the initial planning of the group, surely each one agreed that the community could tolerate different temperaments and could be enriched by various apostolates. As they live close to each other, however, the nervous energy of the one and the quiet thoughtfulness of the other become sources first of guilt feelings and then of resentment. For a time, these feelings may swell subconsciously, but finally they surface. At this point, wariness begins to rule the relationship. The meditative woman feels less free to talk; her philosophizing seems suddenly empty and out of touch with real life, real people, real situations. On her part, the active sister feels like the Martha who could not choose the better part; her activity seems suddenly devoid of the dimension of thoughtfulness or religious motivation. Conversation narrows then to inconsequentials. "I have long noticed that people who talk to those close to them only about what they eat, what they wear, the money they make, the trip they will or will not take next week—such people are of two sorts. They either have no inner life, or their inner life is painful to them, is beset with regret or fear."[4]

If everyone in the community moves backward to a shallower plateau in order to accommodate this wariness and mis-

[4] *Ibid.*, p. 339.

trust, the entire group suffers a loss of community. If, however, one or both of the persons concerned reads the signals correctly and makes a mature response by personal confrontation, the guard can be let down. Talk may be painful, but people are communicating and by that fact they are saying, "I *want* to maintain community." It is difficult not to be moved by that.

When one thread is pulled from the fabric of life and scrutinized by itself, it appears larger than it is. So here. A group of women who want to create religious community most certainly will not spend all their time and psychic energies in introspection. There is something unhealthy in chronic and exaggerated self-analysis.

Not every little crisis or non-verbal tension should be re-solved by confrontation. We must learn to overlook, dismiss, forget small frictions—and not with an attitude of long-suffering but rather with good humor and common sense. Magnifying every trivial difference to bigger-than-life size puts a group in a perpetual state of emergency. Then the old sins occur again: either we try to escape the community through outside interests, or else we express all our emotional energy in the group on picayunes instead of out in the world on service.

Obviously the ability to make the distinction between crisis and friction, and the added ability to engage in confrontation and to assimilate friction demand a certain quality of maturity which is highly sensitive without being hypersensitive. As wide a margin exists between adolescent probing and mature analysis as exists between settling for mediocrity and growing in community.

To grow in community means also to grow in shared leadership, particularly in small groups. Shared decision-making results in shared responsibility.

Natural leadership swings from person to person as different situations arise. One may become a natural leader when questions of budget arise; the leadership may be taken up by another in questions concerning prayer or household. In free groups, leaders follow even as they lead. This is so much the case that the question of leadership is not raised at all in many small new communities. In larger new communities, there is formal leadership often just to the extent of having a business administrator.

How, then, do religious practice obedience? First of all, they are obedient to the Gospels through the Church and according to their conscience. They are not unlike any other Christian woman in this obedience. Further than that, a certain kind of obedience is exercised in community. This obedience is not rendered through adherence to rules, customs, or commands but in response to mutual concern.

The independence of each religious and the acceptance of differences in each other does not rule out concern. To be in community and to be unconcerned is a contradiction. Inconsequentials or purely private actions do not qualify as objects of concern, but consequential actions and attitudes do. In the past, the hour at which a religious retired, the books she read or the television programs she viewed, the letters she wrote—

such private and often unimportant affairs were made the subjects of notice and rule. Perhaps it is in reaction to that kind of super-surveillance that we now tend toward the other extreme of tolerating no concern at all.

A rhetoric has grown up to shame anyone who "butts in." We say, "Live and let live. Whatever she does is her own business." But such principles cannot be absolutely applied regarding *any* human being. We are scandalized when people witness a woman stabbed to death on the street and do nothing.[5] It is also scandalous when religious watch someone to whom they are supposedly committed become entangled in a problem and shrug it off as being no concern of theirs. Unconcern sins against community. And religion. Each person's problems—real and persistent problems—should be a point of concern because, first of all, that person is loved and, second of all, that person affects the whole group.

When we respond to a suggestion made out of concern for us, that response is obedience. The caliber of that obedience far excels obedience in the sense of keeping the schedule or of teaching at the appointed school—the excellence being in the difference between freedom and dependence and, more than that, the difference between community and non-community.

Concern must then be tempered with trust. The lapses into tension and harshness which we all experience do not always signify a falling away from community. If we are responsible for being concerned, we are simultaneously responsible for trusting.

And here the pattern begins to emerge: balance. Balance is the crux of new communities. As compared to the black and

[5] "Why People Don't Help," *Time* (July 18, 1969), p. 66.

white of wrong and right, balance is gray. Some people cannot tolerate this gray country where they must confront and at the same time overlook, concern themselves and yet trust, engage their lives deeply with others and still allow freedom. Because this land is difficult to move through, people may be tempted to chart courses and give specific directions. Such detailing is the pattern of past history in religious life. If today's new communities succumb to that old pattern, history will repeat itself, and we will end up with rigidity again— perhaps new, but rigidity after all.

If communities today, however, are populated with mature women who are free and sincere in their commitment and who can maintain balance in daily living, the number of sisters may dwindle yet more, but the *quality* of community in the world may be unprecedented.

**Date Due**